ASPECTS OF *OTHELLO*

KING ALF

ASPECTS OF
OTHELLO

ARTICLES REPRINTED FROM *SHAKESPEARE SURVEY*

EDITED BY

KENNETH MUIR

EMERITUS PROFESSOR OF ENGLISH LITERATURE
UNIVERSITY OF LIVERPOOL

AND

PHILIP EDWARDS

KING ALFRED PROFESSOR OF ENGLISH LITERATURE
UNIVERSITY OF LIVERPOOL

CAMBRIDGE UNIVERSITY PRESS

CAMBRIDGE

LONDON · NEW YORK · MELBOURNE

Published by the Syndics of the Cambridge University Press
The Pitt Building, Trumpington Street, Cambridge CB2 1RP
Bentley House, 200 Euston Road, London NW1 2DB
32 East 57th Street, New York, NY 10022, USA
296 Beaconsfield Parade, Middle Park, Melbourne 3206, Australia

Library of Congress Catalogue Card Number: 77–560

ISBN 0 521 21499 8 hard covers
ISBN 0 521 29175 5 paperback

This collection first published 1977
Reprinted 1978

Printed in Great Britain at the
University Press, Cambridge

CONTENTS

PLATES

PREFACE

These essays are selected from the annual volumes of *Shakespeare Survey*, the majority from No. 21 (1968) in which *Othello* was the central theme. As Dame Helen Gardner's Retrospect demonstrates, the main critical debate in recent years has centred on the hero's 'nobility', regarded as suspect by T. S. Eliot (1932), F. R. Leavis (1937) and Leo Kirschbaum (1944), and as deeply flawed by Albert Gerard and S. L. Bethell in the present volume, and most recently by Harold Skulsky in *Spirits Finely Touched* (1976). This nobility has been ably defended by Helen Gardner herself in her British Academy Lecture (1956) and by John Bayley in *The Characters of Love* (1960) and it appears to be assumed in varying degrees by most of the contributors to this volume. The debate on Othello's nobility is part of a larger one on the nature of the tragic hero. Many modern critics, in reaction against what they regard as A. C. Bradley's sentimentality, tend to put Shakespeare's heroes in the dock.

Bethell's article, in which Iago is portrayed as a devil luring Othello to damnation, was a valuable demonstration of the function of imagery, Iago's characteristic imagery being transferred to Othello as he succumbed to temptation. Bethell took hints from Caroline Spurgeon's discussion of the play and also from Mikhail M. Morozov's essay, part of which is here reproduced.

Iago's role and character have also been much discussed. Ever since Rymer's complaint in the seventeenth century, and Coleridge's description of one of the soliloquies as the 'motive-hunting of motiveless malignity', critics have discussed whether Iago is merely a stage villain, whether the motives he advances are real to him or not, whether he should be regarded as a Vice, a devil, a Machiavel, a malcontent, a perverted artist, or even a homosexual. Stanley Edgar Hyman in *Iago, Some Approaches to the Illusion of his Motivation* (1970) showed that it was possible to educe evidence from the play itself in support of all these. In the present collection, Leah Scragg, replying to Bernard Spivack's *Shakespeare and the Allegory of Evil*, argues that Iago is closer to medieval devils than to the Vice.

The significance of the Turkish danger to a Jacobean audience and the relevance of James I's *Lepanto* to our understanding of the play is brought out by Emrys Jones. G. R. Hibbard, who also refers to the Turkish danger, distinguishes *Othello* from the other great tragedies.

Some of the discrepancies in the play, which have led to the theory of 'Double Time', are explained by Ned B. Allen as being due to Shakespeare's method of composition, the last three acts, based closely on Cinthio's tale, having been written before the first two. Another essay, on the basic structure of the play, by the Brazilian critic, Barbara Heliodora C. de Mendonça, shows that *Othello*, unlike the other tragedies, has what would normally be regarded as a comic structure. She comments on some of Rymer's objections to the play; and Nigel Alexander takes up Eliot's challenge that Rymer has never been cogently refuted by providing that cogent refutation.

The significance of Othello's colour is not discussed by any of the contributors: for that one must go to G. K. Hunter's *Othello and Colour Prejudice* and Eldred Jones's *Othello's Countrymen* (1965). The portrait of the Moorish Ambassador, reproduced originally in *Shakespeare Survey*, may serve as a reminder of the controversy.

K. M.
P. E.

OTHELLO: A RETROSPECT, 1900–67

BY

HELEN GARDNER

Much of the criticism of *Othello* in this century has been marked by an uneasiness which was first voiced by Bradley. This was partly a consequence of his endeavour to discover and define the 'substance' of a Shakespearian Tragedy. Unable to deny that *Othello* was a masterpiece, and that if we are to distinguish certain of Shakespeare's tragedies as 'the great tragedies' we must place *Othello* among them, he had in honesty to recognize that the vision of the world given by *Othello* did not conform to his conception of the vision of the world that the great tragedies present. It is really impossible to see in the destruction of Othello and Desdemona 'a world travailing for perfection, but bringing to birth, together with glorious good, an evil which it is able to overcome only by self-torture and self-waste'; and Bradley made no attempt to persuade himself or us that at the end of *Othello* we are presented with a world that has, though at a fearful cost, purged itself of evil. On the contrary, he came very near to saying that the impression the course of the play makes on us is of a very different vision of the universe, suggesting that if there are powers outside the wills of men that shape human destinies then these powers are on the side of Iago. Shying away rapidly from this painful notion, he attempted to analyse why 'some readers', while acknowledging the play's power, and even owning that dramatically it is perhaps Shakespeare's greatest triumph, still 'regard it with a certain distaste', or 'hardly allow it a place in their minds beside *Hamlet*, *King Lear* and *Macbeth*'. The distaste he ascribed to the repulsiveness of the subject of sexual jealousy 'treated with Elizabethan fulness and frankness', and to the violence and brutality to which his jealousy drives Othello. The reservation over the play's claim to supreme greatness he ascribed to the 'comparative confinement of the imaginative atmosphere'. '*Othello* has not...the power of dilating the imagination by vague suggestions of huge universal powers working in the world of individual fate and passion.' Compared with the other three 'great tragedies', 'it is, in a sense, less "symbolic"'. It leaves us with the impression that we are not 'in contact with the whole of Shakespeare'; and 'it is perhaps significant in this respect that the hero himself strikes us as having, probably, less of the poet's personality in him than many characters far inferior both as dramatic creations and as men.'

Whether or not Bradley had grounds for ascribing his reservations about *Othello* to other readers in his own day, his unwillingness to grant it supreme greatness has been echoed by critics of very varying schools of thought since he wrote. Many who thought of themselves as opposing Bradley, as well as those who recognized and developed his many brilliant insights, accepted his view that in *Othello* we are not in contact with 'the whole of Shakespeare', and his implication that the hero is not conceived from within. And many have shared his sense that the play lacks universal significance and a larger 'meaning' than any story of terrible individual catastrophe must suggest.

Granville-Barker went so far as to say 'It is a tragedy without meaning, and that is the ultimate horror of it'; and to declare 'It does not so much purge us as fill us with horror and anger'. It must be added that Granville-Barker did not find much 'meaning' in *King Lear*,

I

thinking that the main tragic truth about life that it conveyed was its 'capricious cruelty'. He was, to some extent, reacting as a man of the theatre against Bradley's quasi-philosophic approach to the 'substance' of Shakespearian Tragedy. But those who have followed Bradley in an attempt to seek for the 'meaning' of Shakespeare's tragedies, and have gone beyond Bradley in attempting to show him as progressively exploring human destiny in them, have either tended to ignore *Othello* or to treat it with marked reserve. Thus G. Wilson Knight in his chapter on 'The *Othello* Music' in *The Wheel of Fire* (1930), when attempting to 'expose the underlying thought of the play' owned very honestly that 'Interpretation here is not easy, nor wholly satisfactory'.

As all within *Othello*—save the Iago-theme—is separated, differentiated, solidified, so the play itself seems at first to be divorced from wider issues, a lone thing of meaningless beauty in the Shakespearean universe, solitary, separate, unyielding and chaste as the moon. It is unapproachable, yields itself to no easy mating with our minds.

And in a later chapter, where he compares *Othello* with *Timon of Athens*, though he tries to generalize the play's meaning, it is with provisos:

Ultimately, in so far as *Othello* expresses a universal truth, it must be considered to suggest the inability of love's faith to weather the conditions of this world...This meaning is not obvious in *Othello*: but it is seen to be implicit on the analogy of other plays. This general theme, in *Othello* projected into definite persons and events, is the very theme to be expressed later in *Timon of Athens*. There a change has taken. place. *Othello's* figures are first men and women, and only second symbols; the plot is first a story, second a philosophic argument. In *Timon of Athens* the reverse obtains. Timon is first a symbol, second a human being; the play is primarily an argument or parable, only secondarily forced, as it best may, to assume some correspondence with the forms and events of human affairs... *Othello* and *Timon of Athens* are together concerned with the recurrent Shakespeare 'hate-theme': the one is the most concretely projected into human symbols, the other the most universal and profound dramatic statement of this Shakespearean philosophy.

The comparison, as has more than once been pointed out, which equates Desdemona as a symbol with 'the men of Athens—that is mankind—' hardly does justice to what is the source of the keenest pain and the deepest consolation that *Othello* affords: that Desdemona, unlike Timon's friends, is not false and that at the close Othello knows this. Wilson Knight's obvious preference for the 'mighty parable of *Timon of Athens*' over the 'consummate artistry of *Othello*' echoes Bradley's statement that *Othello* is less 'symbolic' than the other tragedies; and his sense of the inadequacy of the 'universal truth' he finds in it to express the truth of the play Shakespeare actually wrote goes to confirm Granville-Barker's view that *Othello* is not a 'spiritual tragedy' and that it has no 'meaning', if by the 'meaning' of a tragedy we understand some statement about the nature of the universe and mankind's role in it which the tragedy expresses or symbolizes. Writers such as D. G. James in *The Dream of Learning* (1951), concerned to assert that the imagination is an 'instrument of truth', an exploration of the nature of reality, make a passing reference to Iago as 'the inexplicable but indisputable evil in our mortal nature'— for Iago can, in a way, be allegorized—and rapidly pass from *Hamlet* to *King Lear*, both of which appear to invite the kind of interpretation that *Othello* appears to resist. From *King Lear* they can move to the Last Plays which have proved so congenial to the taste of this century and so amenable to interpretative criticism. Meanwhile *Othello* remains awkwardly and obstinately there: between *Hamlet* and *King Lear* if we wish to trace Shakespeare's development as a tragic artist, and roughly contemporary with *Measure for Measure* if we are trying to plot the whole movement of his mind. Wilson Knight's complaint that 'its thought does not readily mesh with our thought' reflects a genuine dilemma for many twentieth-century critics, who find themselves confronted with a work of obviously supreme artistic power and beauty which does not satisfy their characteristic concerns and strongly resists their characteristic methods. From Johnson onwards the striking merit of *Othello* has always been recognized to lie in the individuality and vitality of the characters and the closeness of the interplay among them, the clarity and concentration of the plot. The persons of the drama are not reducible to symbols, and the play cannot be regarded as an attempt to objectify obscure and dark feelings that have not found full and clear expression, which it is left to the genius of the critic to expose. The 'admirable equilibrium' of the powers of Shakespeare's mind which Coleridge[1] saw in *Othello* defeats the interpreter seeking for a reality that the poet has been able to present only more or less adequately in symbolic form. A preference for *Timon of Athens*—a play rarely performed and thought by some scholars and critics to be more a draft than a finished play—over *Othello* is only an extreme example of a taste characteristic of this century for 'late works' over the works of an artist's maturity, and for 'giant art' rather than fully realized creations: the late quartets of Beethoven rather than the Rasoumovsky quartets, Michelangelo's *Pietà* in Florence rather than his *Pietà* in St Peter's.

Having confessed his reservations as to the 'meaning' and the stature of *Othello*, Bradley turned to analysis of the characters. Though much that he says is true, and one is struck by his care to take all the evidence into account, his studies of Othello and Desdemona lack conviction. He writes in a mixture of the fusty and of fustian of Othello's romantic nobility and Desdemona's sweetness. But his study of Iago is perhaps his masterpiece. His obvious fascination with Iago anticipates the fascination later critics have felt, and studies as various as William Empson's 'Honest in *Othello*'[2], Bernard Spivack's *Shakespeare and the Allegory of Evil* (1958), and W. H. Auden's 'The Joker in the Pack'[3] develop, as Empson and Spivack freely own, from Bradley's insights. Empson, from Bradley's comment on 'Iago's superficial good-nature, the kind of good-nature that wins popularity and is often taken as a sign, not of a good digestion, but of a good heart', went on to a brilliant discussion of Iago as 'a critique on an unconscious pun' on the word 'honest'. Spivack, starting from Bradley's comment on the curious difference between the motives that Iago ascribes to himself, which are passionate motives, and the coldness with which he utters them, develops his conception of Iago as the stage figure of the Vice (enemy of Mankind, but compelled by the old homiletic tradition to declare himself evil and pay tribute to the virtues he exists to destroy) imperfectly naturalised as 'his Moorship's ancient'. Auden's picture of Iago as the 'practical joker' develops from Bradley's subtle recognition of a kind of complicity between Shakespeare the tragic poet and Iago 'the amateur of tragedy', as Hazlitt called him, the 'inarticulate poet' of Swinburne. He substitutes for the amoral artist of Bradley a bogeyman of our own day: the amoral experimental scientist. Bradley, with a flash of genius, pointed to 'the curious analogy between the early stages of dramatic composition and those soliloquies in which Iago broods over his plot, drawing at first only an outline, puzzled how to fix more than the main idea, and gradually seeing it develop and clarify as he works upon it or lets it work'.

But Bradley saw, as some later critics have not,[4] that 'the tragedian in real life was not the equal of the tragic poet. His psychology, as we shall see, was at fault at a critical point...and so his catastrophe came out wrong and his piece was ruined'. Bradley recognized that in the last two acts the situation moves beyond Iago's control and that his scurrying about in the dark is peripheral to us, absorbed in the fates of Othello and Desdemona.

However fascinating Iago may be, it is Othello's tragedy that we are asked to contemplate. For all his activity Iago is essentially parasitic on Othello. In the dramatic economy of the play he exists for Othello's sake, not Othello for his. But while (apart from a few aberrant voices taking Iago's claims to promotion as well-founded and thus accepting him as wronged, and others who curiously regard this congenital liar as in some way representing a 'true view of life') criticism in this century has on the whole agreed to see in him the spirit of negation and cynicism, an embodiment of 'the destructive element', there has been no such agreement over Othello. Influential voices, from T. S. Eliot in 1927 onwards,[5] have qualified or flatly opposed the traditional view of Othello as, in Johnson's words, 'magnanimous, artless, and credulous, boundless in his confidence, ardent in his affection, inflexible in his resolution, and obdurate in his revenge'; and have contraverted Johnson's praise of 'the gradual progress which *Iago* makes in the Moor's conviction, and the circumstances which he employs to inflame him' as 'artfully natural' A tendency to qualify the conception of Othello as a heroic figure, calling out a passionate sympathy which survives his appalling deed, reached its zenith in F. R. Leavis's famous onslaught on Bradley's Othello, which gave us, in place of Johnson's and Coleridge's Othello, an Othello whose pride, egoism, lack of self-knowledge and 'awareness', shown by his indulgence in inflated rhetoric, make him an easy prey to Iago (also scaled down), responding 'with a promptness that couldn't be improved upon' to 'Iago's "communications"'.[6] Throughout this period the traditional view held its own and was finely stated, notably by Middleton Murry, Peter Alexander and J. I. M. Stewart. It laboured under difficulties since it was accused of sentimentality—a fatal charge among the young, anxious not to be taken in; though, since tragedy is concerned with human suffering, it might be thought that an excess of sympathy is a lesser defect in a critic than a lack of it. When in 1954 I was invited to give the annual Shakespeare Lecture by the British Academy and chose as my subject 'The Noble Moor',[7] I thought of myself as fighting a stubborn rearguard action alongside such veterans as Dover Wilson, whose long introduction to his edition of the play in 1957 powerfully argued the traditional view. It now appears that I was conducting a forward skirmish, for two impressive studies of the play in this decade, John Bayley's in *The Characters of Love* in 1960, and John Holloway's in *The Story of the Night* in the following year, brilliantly restated that the central subject of Othello is love, and jealousy, which is a disease of love. Mr Bayley challenged the conception that 'awareness' is the prime human virtue, commenting on our modern undervaluing of achievement; and attacked the notion that Shakespeare was concerned with 'placing' his characters, declaring on the contrary that he endows all of them 'with the greatest possible freedom to be themselves'. Dr Holloway's chapter is a fine example of the value of an historical approach in clearing away obstacles to our discovering what a work of art 'offers for our experience' today. Both Mr Bayley and Dr Holloway were attacking some basic assumptions in Dr Leavis's criticism of the play; but Dr Holloway went further and in a long and closely argued appendix examined Dr Leavis's anti-Bradley essay, to vindicate Johnson's view that Othello was very far from 'responding with promptness', and to show that in his polemic against Bradley's Othello Dr Leavis had neglected Shakespeare's.[8]

I think Dr Holloway perhaps was a little too ready to declare that certain Elizabethan conceptions are outmoded today, and I am far from sure that his 'modern reader' can be equated with all modern readers. The conflict of attitudes on such subjects as 'jealousy, fidelity, chastity, the quality of desire between a man and a woman, the illicit or degenerate forms of it, the rights that lovers have over each other, the proper response to amorous treachery' is one reason for the conflict of views about the play and its hero. We can all accept, because it is so wholly dead, the notion of Order and Hierarchy as a universal Law of Nature and the basis of a proper social order, and find that this gives us a perspective from which to interpret the History Plays. The notion that fidelity is something we look for in those we love, and something we bind ourselves to when we love another person, is very much more than an idea which once had validity but is now merely intellectually apprehensible. It is an idea which is still passionately held, though one would hardly guess so from reading much modern fiction. I am not sure that 'the notion of the equality of men and women in matters of love' is generally held by the 'modern reader'; and even a casual reading of police-court news at home or *faits divers* abroad can make us question the notion, to quote Empson, that 'the advent of contraceptives has taken a lot of strain off the topic' of adultery. But Dr Holloway's discussion of Othello as 'a prince by birth, and only one below a prince by his office' and of Elizabethan ideals of the conduct and speech required and expected of such a man most interestingly combines with Mr Bayley's stress on him as a man of achievement, a kind of hero that modern novelists and dramatists conspicuously find uninteresting.

Othello is Shakespeare's one full portrait of a professional soldier, a man to whom war is not 'the sport of kings' and involved in politics, but a complete way of life. He is a man of action and heroic in his deeds; but he is also a man on whom the safety of the civil order depends, capable not only of risking his own life and outfacing fear but also of assuming responsibility for the lives of others. Self-confidence and decisiveness are pre-requisites for success in such a career. Shakespeare has wonderfully depicted in him the blend of personal courage and authority that ideally belongs to the 'General Officer', and makes other men willing to follow him into 'the imminent deadly breach'. It is difficult for those whose responsibilities for the lives of others do not demand of them the capacity for swift decision and action[9] to appreciate the qualities of those who have to act on disciplined instinct and make decisions in a flash: the surgeon confronted with something his diagnosis had not led him to expect, the general when the unexpected irrupts into his planned campaign. This demands a certain simplicity that the subtle and introspective are only too ready to equate with stupidity. They tend to dismiss those who act from the depth of their nature, and by an intuitive sense of the situation, as dull and uninteresting. But in addition to the stress of modern literature on the value of self-consciousness and self-criticism, the stigmatizing of Othello as 'unaware' had an obvious relation to the appalling catastrophe of the First World War, and the blow that the image of the professional soldier received from the senseless carnage in Flanders. It became axiomatic in the twenties and thirties that professional soldiers were stupid. Even Wyndham Lewis, who sympathized with the Lion against the Fox, saw Othello as a kind of dazed, unhappy bull with Iago as a clever matador dancing round him. In the revulsion against war it became very difficult to entertain the idea

5

that Shakespeare's soldier heroes were heroes to him. 'Every man', said Johnson, 'thinks meanly of himself for not having been a soldier, or not having been at sea.'[10] As a great poetic dramatist Shakespeare heightened all the elements in the story he dramatized. His subject being sexual love and marriage, he heightened in every way the contrast of masculine and feminine, to show love as the discovery of union in opposites. Othello's absolute soldiership is the symbol of his entire masculinity. It is a symbol that has lost much of its force to many today, as has the concept of distinctively masculine virtues.

It could hardly be expected that *Othello* could escape a 'Christian interpretation' which neither Johnson nor Coleridge, whose personal commitment to Christian beliefs cannot be doubted, thought it proper to read into it. Johnson, who censured Pope for 'the illaudable singularity of treating suicide with respect', makes no comment on the suicide of Othello any more than he does on the suicides of Romeo and Juliet, or on the Roman deaths of Brutus, Antony and Cleopatra. He was content to accept these actions as 'natural', and as the end of the story in this world. Of all the suicides in Shakespeare, Othello's is the most defensible morally. It is not an escape from an intolerable life but an act of justice. Anticipating the inevitable verdict of the Venetian court and accepting it fully, he declares by his act his responsibility for what he has done, and stigmatizes himself as a criminal. As he sacrificed Desdemona to his ideal of faithfulness, now that he sees the truth he sacrifices himself, to 'die upon a kiss'. No other ending can leave them together; as they are truly together in the value they both set upon loyalty in love as a supreme virtue. I am sorry that Mr Bayley should write that Othello 'is sure his suicide will cut him off from the last hope of mercy', and add 'To ignore this is to ignore the convictions of religion'.[11] This is to read into Othello's final speech what is not there. His sense of eternal separation when he and Desdemona will 'meet at compt' comes earlier, when he sees himself as murderer and her as martyred victim. But in the last speech this sense of separation is lost in the final sense of union, typified by Othello's last words: 'a kiss'. Verdi, who had the advantage of writing for a stage that employed a final curtain, knew how *Othello* ended. He brought a hint of the great love-duet of the first act back as Othello entered the marriage-chamber where Desdemona lay sleeping; he brought it back in all its beauty and nobility at the close with the last phrase of his opera: *un altro bacio*. The play must disclose to us at the end that the world of Othello and Desdemona is not Iago's world. It could not do this if Othello, like Iago, were taken off, a prisoner, to face trial and execution. This would be intolerable, and dramatically inept. The play must end by justifying Othello's cry: 'My life upon her faith', and leave us the final image of Othello, Desdemona and Emilia for ever separated by death, for ever united in our imagination.

When Eliot said that he had 'never read a more convincing exposure of human weakness—of universal human weakness—than the last great speech of Othello', he was taking this speech as only the greatest example of something he deplored in other Elizabethan dramatists as well as in Shakespeare: self-dramatization by the heroes at the moment of death, the adoption of an 'aesthetic rather than a moral attitude'. He took Othello as the most striking example (which indeed he is) of a man on the brink of eternity 'endeavouring to escape reality' by '*cheering himself up*'. Eliot owns that Othello 'takes in the spectator'. He does not make clear whether he 'took in' his author also: whether Shakespeare is deliberately exposing self-deception and human weakness in his hero, or, himself deceived, is presenting such an attitude as 'noble' and only

6

unconsciously revealing human weakness. I think the implication of the whole essay is that it is Shakespeare who is exposing his own false values, and that it is Shakespeare's inadequate view of life and death rather than Othello's that we should censure. Later critics who have fastened on this speech as an example of Othello's self-dramatization have shown less awareness than Eliot of Othello's likeness here to other tragic figures who, in place of humbly and penitently preparing themselves to meet their Judge, look back over their past lives and re-assert the values they have lived by. Hamlet is forced by the potent poison to leave his justification to Horatio; Lear is prevented by extremity of weakness and grief from speaking; but Antony who, like Eliot's Hamlet, has 'made a pretty considerable mess of things', even bungling his own suicide, and Coriolanus, whose end is singularly unheroic, also assert in the face of death that their life had glory. Othello is allowed to make at length his *apologia pro vita sua*; and if in so doing he 'cheers himself up' he cheers us up too. Because the deed of horror is deferred in this play until the final scene, and the spectacle of Desdemona dead before our eyes is so heart-rending, the self-assertion of the hero must be fuller than other rallyings of the hero's essential nature in catastrophe, reminding us of the twin values of love and loyalty by which he has tried to live.

Something of the same kind of failure to recognize dramatic values, and dramatic necessities lurks behind Wilson Knight's reservations over the 'Othello music'. Finding as characteristic of the play two worlds of imagery, Othello's and Iago's, and pointing to the central confusion, when Iago takes over at moments the language of Othello and Othello descends into the animal world of Iago, he discovers in Othello's characteristic speech something 'over-decorated, highly-coloured' and declares that 'there is something sentimental in it' and that 'at moments of great tension, the Othello style fails of a supreme effect'.[12] He takes as his example four lines from Othello's last speech and compares them with an outburst of grief from Macduff. This is again to ignore dramatic circumstance. Othello is attempting to present himself to the world's judgement. The last speech presents a parallel, in terrible circumstances, to the speech in which he defended himself before the Senate in the first act. It is by a mighty effort of self-control that Othello here achieves the 'restrained melodic beauty' which is compared unfavourably with an outburst of natural grief at hearing grievous news by a minor character. The discipline of a life that has been lived at danger-point and has taken its value from service to the state is behind the control with which Othello here attempts a summation of what we have seen, without extenuation and without indulgence in the hysterical self-loathing he has shown earlier in the scene.

A rather different assessment of the characteristic speech of Othello and Iago is given by Wolfgang Clemen.[13] Commenting on the highly personal nature of Othello's imagery, drawn from a wide experience, and noting that he 'is almost always talking of himself, his life and his feelings', he sees Othello's imagery as serving to 'express his own emotions and his own nature'; adding 'with the innocence and frankness characteristic of strong natures who live within themselves he always takes *himself* as the point of departure'. Imagery, on the other hand, is not natural to Iago, who is always 'looking for comparisons'. He likes 'general statements' whereas Othello 'characteristically never discusses general human values'. What other writers have seen as Othello's 'egoism', lack of intellectual power, and 'sentimentality', Clemen sees as generous frankness, and sincerity and integrity of emotion: he 'does not measure his imagery by the effect which it is to have upon others; he speaks what is in his heart'. The strength of Clemen's book is that his concern with imagery goes along with a sense of dramatic reality and dramatic possibility. It is this that is lacking in Robert B. Heilman's very full study, *Magic in the Web* (1956), which presents an Othello as secretly unsure of himself, displaying 'immaturity, histrionism, and incompleteness of love', a 'romantic personality that has found a military outlet' in 'a stoicism that can develop into toughness and ruthlessness'.[14] His 'military virtues...hardly equip him for a demanding intimate personal relationship'. It is difficult to see how any actor could present this 'secretly unsure' Othello as he declaims Othello's magnificently confident lines; or how, while enchanting the Senate (and the audience) with his account of his 'travel's history', he could manage to convey to them the immaturity of his romantic view of his experience.

These approaches to *Othello*, even when apparently most hostile to Bradley, are in the tradition of Bradley, who combined the search for meaning with acute psychological analysis, and with recognition of 'dominant imagery' in the plays he studied. Bradley's main weakness as a critic of tragedy lay in his defective feeling for the stage. He took insufficient account of the distinction between characterization in a novel and characterization in a play. The novelist creates characters that have come to life in our imagination; the dramatist creates characters that an actor is to bring to life on the stage. There is a penumbra of uncertainty surrounding dramatically conceived characters which calls upon the actor's imagination and gives scope for his art. They are always, even in soliloquy, presenting themselves to us, creating themselves as characters expressive of a personality which it is the actor's business to convey. To be dramatic, they must to some extent dramatize themselves, whether by hyperbole, or, as more often today, by understatement. In our actual encounters with other people—as distinct from our encounter with them in memory, imagination, and reflection—we are often surprised, and made aware of the mystery of human personality. In the same way, fully dramatic characters impress us with a present reality and 'tease us out of thought'. The acts and speeches of men, how they present themselves to the world, are the dramatist's main concern, not their motives. This does not mean that characterization and psychological consistency are less required of the dramatist than the novelist; only that they reveal themselves in rather different ways. Bradley's overmastering concern with 'why' conflicts with the dramatist's absorption in 'how'. To make discussion of motives our prime concern is to neglect the glory of drama, its power to present before our eyes and ears an image of human life that convinces us of its truth even while it surprises us. The anti-Bradleyans I have mentioned have switched their interest from 'Why does Iago act as he does?' to 'Why does Othello believe Iago?' They are unwilling to 'rest in uncertainties, mysteries, doubts, without any irritable reaching after fact and reason'; and to accept that with dramatic characters we must be 'content with half-knowledge'. For they come before us with a physical reality that is not wholly amenable to intellectual analysis, and while we dissect our 'meddling intellect' may well murder.

Further, unlike as they are to Bradley in their interpretation of Othello's character, the moralists who find the root of the tragedy in his 'pride', or his 'egoism', or 'immaturity' are, like Bradley, shrinking from the central subject, the tragic fact that *Othello* presents. It is more comforting to rise from reading[15] *Othello* with the assurance that persons of 'greater awareness' can avoid tragic disaster than to see Othello as Raleigh saw him: suffering 'for his very virtues', a man 'carried off his feet, wave-drenched and blinded by the passion of love', and to feel in the 'compulsive course' of the play's swift onward movement the strength of 'the tides that bear men with them'. Thus 'we make trifles of terrors, ensconcing ourselves into seeming knowledge when we should submit ourselves to an unknown fear'.

The assault on Bradley by Levin Schücking and Edgar Elmer Stoll was much more radical. Both can be treated as historical critics, insisting that we interpret Shakespeare in the light of Elizabethan stage conventions. But their fundamental importance—and this is particularly true of Stoll—is that they gave primacy to dramatic values. Like all persons applying correctives, they overstated; and for the subtle psychologist of Bradley they can be accused of substituting a Shakespeare who was simply a seeker for crude dramatic effects. This charge does, I think, remain against Schücking and, though less so, against Stoll in his original study; but in his last treatment of the play, in *Art and Artifice in Shakespeare* (1933), Stoll's basic contention (that Othello, whom he accepts as not naturally jealous, becomes insanely jealous through 'a mechanical device'; the convention that the slanderer is always believed[16]) seems less important than the strength of his response to dramatic tension and dramatic poetry, and his recognition that the core of the play is, in De Quincey's words, 'the dire necessity of loving without limit one whom the heart pronounces to be unworthy of that love'. This is recognized by J. I. M. Stewart,[17] who, having shrewdly observed against Stoll that the very fact that the convention of the 'slanderer believed' was so widespread pointed to its reflecting some general truth about human nature, owned that we 'are indebted to him' for calling our attention to 'the element of artifice, of boldly unrealistic devices used to significant ends'.

Stoll diminishes the Iago of Bradley by making him a piece of dramatic machinery, as Leavis diminishes him by making Othello so easy a victim. Others, unwilling to accept that Shakespeare was not interested in psychological truth, or that Iago is not a most powerfully imagined and impressively convincing tempter, have turned from analysis of the two individual characters separately to find in their association an 'archetypal' meaning. Thus Maud Bodkin thought that Iago's power over Othello came from his injecting into his mind the 'half-truths that Othello's romantic vision ignored, but of which his mind held secret knowledge', and wrote of the reader in the same way 'experiencing the romantic values represented in the hero, and recognizing, in a manner secretly, the complementary truths projected in the figure of Iago'. Empson echoed her, thinking that there is 'a certain sting of truth in Iago's claim to honesty, even in the broadest sense of being somehow truer than Othello to the facts of life'. The difficulty of such a view is that it ignores the fact of Desdemona's fidelity and unswerving love. Her presence in the play flatly contradicts the supposed 'insights' of Iago: his generalizations break down on the rock of her truth. As John Bayley observed, Iago's 'outlook is simple, brutal, and dull': it is proved false by Emilia as well as by Desdemona—and even by the pathetic constancy of Roderigo in his hopeless pursuit. Yet there is still a sense in which the polar opposites—Othello and Iago—are inseparable, as Hamlet is inseparable from his father's Ghost. Perhaps Stewart, while giving full value to the characters of the play as natural and realistically conceived, best expresses this in seeing in the play a symbolic presentation of the conflicting forces in the single human psyche: 'Othello *is* the human soul as it strives to be and the Iago *is* that which corrodes or subverts it from within.' Picking up a fine *aperçu* from Middleton Murry, he went on to see in Iago 'an imaginative device for making visible something in the nature of time', finding 'something inward about the oddity of the time-scheme of *Othello*', on whose oddity indeed the whole success of Iago's 'plotting' of the tragedy depends. 'It is as if Iago only wins out because of

9

something fundamentally treacherous in time, some flux and reflux in it which is inimical to life and love.'[18] A view which sees in *Othello* the tragic sense that there is something in the very nature of our temporal existence that defeats our highest human needs and aspirations, and that 'To live your life is not as simple as to cross a field',[19] seems more adequate to Shakespeare's play than an attempt to find the root of the disaster in flaws in Othello's nature that made him an easy prey to Iago. It is perilous to garner up one's heart in the heart of another human being, and whoever does so loses control of his own destiny. Passion has its ebbs and flows. The attempt to found the social bond of marriage on passionate love is a great adventure of the human spirit—an attempt to unite contrary values—that brings with it a possibility of agony that those who seek for no such unity in their experience do not risk.

© HELEN GARDNER 1968

NOTES

1. '*Lear* is the most tremendous effort of Shakespeare as a poet; *Hamlet* as a philosopher or meditater; and *Othello* is the union of the two. There is something gigantic and unformed in the former two; but in the latter, everything assumes its due place and proportion, and the whole mature powers of his mind are displayed in admirable equilibrium' (*Table Talk*, 24 December 1822).

2. See *The Structure of Complex Words* (1951), chapter 11.

3. See *The Dyer's Hand* (1963), pp. 246–72.

4. A great many odd things have been said about the action of *Othello*; but I think I would award the prize (though the competition is severe) for the most untrue statement about the play to Mr Auden: 'Any consideration of the Tragedy of Othello must be primarily occupied, not with its official hero but with its villain. I cannot think of any other play in which only one character performs personal actions—all the *deeds* are Iago's—and all the others without exception only exhibit behaviour. In marrying each other, Othello and Desdemona have performed a deed, but this took place before the play begins.'

5. See 'Shakespeare and the Stoicism of Seneca' (1927), reprinted in *Selected Essays 1917–1932* (1932).

6. See 'Diabolic Intellect and the Noble Hero: or the Sentimentalist's Othello', *Scrutiny* (1937); reprinted in *The Common Pursuit* (1952).

7. See *Proceedings of the British Academy*, vol. XLI (1956).

8. In the same year (1961), and independently, Barbara Everett took issue with Dr Leavis from a rather different point of view, concentrating on his statement that 'The essential traitor is within the gates...the mind

that undoes him (Othello) is his own'. See *The Critical Quarterly*, Summer 1961. Miss Everett's view of Shakespeare's mode of characterization and of his attitude to his characters is very close to Mr Bayley's.

9. Professors deciding whether to award a first or second class and tutors advising their pupils can discharge their responsibilities in the calm of thought.

10. The whole conversation is very instructive. Boswell replied: 'Lord Mansfield does not.' 'Sir', riposted Johnson, 'if Lord Mansfield were in a company of General Officers and Admirals who have been in service, he would shrink; he'd wish to creep under the table.' To which Boswell replied: 'No, he'd think he could try them all.' But Johnson persisted: 'Yes, if he could catch them; but they'd try him sooner. No, Sir; were Socrates and Charles the Twelfth of Sweden both present in any company, and Socrates to say "Follow me, and hear a lecture in philosophy;" and Charles, laying his hand on his sword, to say "Follow me, and dethrone the Czar;" a man would be ashamed to follow Socrates. Sir, the impression is universal; yet it is strange.' Boswell, *Life of Johnson*, ed. G. Birkbeck Hill, revised L. F. Powell, (1924), III, 265–6.

11. A rigorously Christian interpretation would see Othello's suicide as only the culmination of his erroneous attempt to find ultimate value in the love of another human being. But to accept this as Othello's error is surely to make nonsense of the whole play. The only critic I know who suggests that in loving Desdemona Othello re-enacts the Fall of Man is Arthur Sewell in *Character and Society in Shakespeare* (1951). It seems to me so eccentric to hold that Desdemona and Iago 'belong to the same world, the same Venice', and to

ignore that Othello has chosen to belong to Venice long before the play begins, that I find it difficult to accept this view of Othello as corrupted by his love for Desdemona as well as by his 'acceptance of Iago's values'. I cannot feel that the message of *Othello* is 'Stay celibate and you won't get into trouble'; or that Othello ever accepts Iago's values.

12. But Wilson Knight, while feeling some dissatisfaction over the '*Othello* music', still finds the Othello of the last scene 'a nobly tragic figure' and says 'at the end we know that Othello's fault is simplicity alone...His simple faith in himself endures: and at the end, he takes just pride in recalling his honourable service.'

13. See *The Development of Shakespeare's Imagery* (1951) pp. 120–1, 128–9; first published in German in 1936, the same year as Caroline Spurgeon's *Shakespeare's Imagery*. The book was extensively revised and altered for its translation, by the author, into English.

14. See pp. 137–41. The expected comparison to Shakespeare's presentation is supplied. Othello's ruthlessness is 'akin to the hardness of spirit of the good man gone self-righteous, a recurrent theme of George Eliot's'. It might be said of T. S. Eliot that he thought all drama aspired (or should aspire) to the condition of *Everyman*, and of Leavis and those who follow him that they think all fictions, whether narrative or dramatic, aspire (or should aspire) to the condition of *Middlemarch*. I am struck by the assumption that the military virtues unfit men for the demands of marriage. Does experience support the view that soldiers make less good husbands than professors?

15. I say 'from reading', because I cannot believe anyone leaves the theatre, even after an inadequate performance, with this feeling.

16. Though perhaps not as odd as Auden's neglect to notice that Othello commits a murder, it is still very odd that Stoll should declare that in *Othello* we see 'the generous and unsuspicious hero, believing a person whom he does not love or really know and has no right reason to trust, to the point of disbelieving persons whom he loves and has every reason to trust' and should refer to the failure of 'doubter and doubted...despite long acquaintance, to enjoy any knowledge of each other's character'. It is surely a main *donnée* of the play that Othello and Iago have been long acquainted, and that though Othello loves Desdemona they are strangers to each other.

17. *Character and Motive in Shakespeare* (1949).

18. He might have noted that in a play roughly contemporary with *Othello* Time is spoken of in words that might apply to Iago as 'envious and calumniating' (*Troilus and Cressida*, III, iii, 174).

19. A Russian proverb, used by Pasternak in Zhivago's poem on Hamlet. See *Dr Zhivago* (1958), p. 467.

"EGREGIOUSLY AN ASS": THE DARK SIDE OF THE MOOR. A VIEW OF OTHELLO'S MIND

BY

ALBERT GERARD

It is through the malice of this earthly air, that only by being guilty of
Folly does mortal man in many cases arrive at the perception of sense.

HERMAN MELVILLE

There are three schools of *Othello* criticism. The most recent of these is the symbolic school, chiefly represented by G. Wilson Knight and J. I. M. Stewart, who have endeavoured to explain away the difficulties inherent in the traditional psychological interpretation of the Moor by turning the play into a mythic image of the eternal struggle between good and evil, embodied in the noble aspirations of Othello and the cunning cynicism of Iago.[1] This school arose in part as a reaction to an attitude mainly exemplified by Stoll, though already initiated by Rymer and Bridges, according to whom this tragedy ought to be treated as a purely dramatic phenomenon, created by Shakespeare for the sake of sensation and emotional effect.[2] The third school is the traditional school of naturalistic interpretation; it branches off into two main streams: the Romantic critics, from Coleridge to Bradley, take Othello at his own valuation, and seem to experience no difficulty in assuming that his greatness of mind should blind him to Iago's evil purposes; more recent students, however, tend to have a more realistic view of the Moor and to stress the flaws in his character: T. S. Eliot speaks of *bovarysme* and self-dramatization, while his homonym, G. R. Elliott, asserts that the main tragic fault in Othello is pride.[3]

One way to solve this crux of Shakespeare criticism is to use the inductive method recently advocated by R. S. Crane, and look for the "particular shaping principle (which) we must suppose to have governed Shakespeare's construction of the tragedy" through "a comparison of the material data of action, character, and motive supplied to Shakespeare by Cinthio's *novella* with what happened to these in the completed play".[4] By analysing the way Shakespeare used (or neglected) some of the data provided by Cinthio, the way he transmuted a vaudevillesque melodrama into one of the unforgettable tragedies in world literature, we may perhaps hope to gain a fresh insight into what he saw in it, why he was attracted by it and what he meant to do with it.

ERRING BARBARIAN AND CREDULOUS FOOL

This method is the one already applied by H. B. Charlton in his Clark Lectures at Cambridge, 1946–7.[5] According to Charlton, one of the most significant alterations made by Shakespeare to Cinthio's story consists in the strengthened emphasis upon the difference in manners and outlook between Desdemona and her husband. Though this motif is barely alluded to by Cinthio, Shakespeare seized on the hint and expanded it to meaningful proportions. The most con-

12

spicuous, though, admittedly, the most superficial, aspect of this difference is the complexion of the Moor. In the original tale, there is only one allusion to Othello's blackness. In the play, his black skin and thick lips are mentioned time and again. As it is obviously impossible to retain the Romantic view that Othello is not a real Negro,[6] we can safely assume that the blackness of the Moor, though it did not strike the Italian writer, appealed to the imagination of Shakespeare, who found it significant in a way that Cinthio, probably, could not even conceive.

Where is this significance to be found? I do not feel very happy about Charlton's suggestion that Shakespeare wanted to stress the physical and psychological antinomies between Othello and Desdemona because "the situation created by the marriage of a man and a woman who are widely different in race, in tradition and in customary way of life" was, at the time, "a particular problem of immediate contemporary interest". There does not seem to be any compelling evidence that such a problem was especially acute in the early seventeenth century, so that it may be worth while to try another line of interpretation.

In *The Dream of Learning*, D. G. James has made excellent use of the changes which Shakespeare introduced into the personality of Belleforest's Hamlet so as to make it plausible that this young Danish chieftain should appear to all ages as the embodiment of the man of thought, or, to use a more up-to-date expression, of the intellectual. Now, if Shakespeare turned Hamlet into an intellectual, it is equally true that he reversed the process in his handling of Othello. Not only does Iago call the Moor an "ass" and a "fool", not only does Othello concur with this unfavourable view in the last stages of the action, but the action itself is hinged upon Othello's obtuseness. This is quite palpable in III, iii, and we may be confident that if Partridge had seen *Othello* performed, he would have felt, at that moment, like jumping on to the stage and telling the Moor not to be an ass. Othello's muddle-headedness on this occasion is so extreme that critics like Rymer, Bridges and Stoll have indeed found it incredible and psychologically untrue. We might draw up a formidable list of Othello's glaring mistakes as exemplified in this scene. A few examples will suffice.

First, he must know that Iago wanted to become his lieutenant: he ought to be suspicious of his accusations against Cassio. Even though he believes, like everybody else, in Iago's honesty,[7] he must know that his Ancient has a vulgar mind, and he should not allow his imagination to be impressed by Iago's obscene pictures of Desdemona. It is also remarkable that he does not try to argue the matter with Iago; in the early stages of his evolution, he simply proclaims his faith in Desdemona's chastity, but he cannot find any sensible argument with which to counter Iago's charges. It is true that he asks for some material proof of his wife's treachery, but he never bothers to inquire about the value of the "evidence" produced by Iago. Finally, once he is convinced of Desdemona's unfaithfulness, surely the next step is to go and discuss things with her or with Cassio; this he never does. Few people would make such a hopeless mess of the situation.

Whereas Shakespeare had keyed Hamlet's intelligence to the highest possible pitch, he deliberately stressed Othello's lack of intellectual acumen, psychological insight, and even plain common sense. In the play, Othello's negroid physiognomy is simply the emblem of a difference that reaches down to the deepest levels of personality. If Hamlet is over-civilized, Othello is, in actual fact, what Iago says he is, a "barbarian" (I, iii, 363).

Othello's fundamental barbarousness becomes clear when we consider his religious beliefs. His superficial acceptance of Christianity should not blind us to his fundamental paganism. To quote again from Charlton's study, "when his innermost being is stirred to its depths", he has "gestures and phrases" which belong rather "to dim pagan cults than to any form of Christian worship". These primitive elements receive poetic and dramatic shape in the aura of black magic which at times surrounds Othello. Though Brabantio is wide of the mark when he charges the Moor with resorting to witchcraft in order to seduce his daughter, it is nevertheless true, as Mark Van Doren has said, that "an infusion of magic does tincture the play",[8] and it comes to the fore in the handkerchief episode. The magic in *Othello* results from his acquiescence in obscure savage beliefs. It is an elemental force at work in the soul of the hero. It helps to build up the Moor as a primitive type.

Here again, we wonder why Shakespeare was attracted by such a hero. A twentieth-century dramatist might be interested in the clash of two cultures, which occurs in the mind of Othello. But though this aspect of the situation is not altogether ignored by Shakespeare, his main concern lies in another direction. The fact is that this tragedy of deception, self-deception, unjustified jealousy and criminal revenge demanded such a hero.

The crime-columns of the newspapers teach us that the people who murder their wives out of jealousy are generally mental defectives. Ordinary sensible people simply cannot believe that such a crime should deserve such a punishment. It was impossible for Shakespeare to take a subnormal type as a hero for his tragedy. Tennessee Williams could do it, I suppose, but not Shakespeare, because the Renaissance tradition required that tragedy should chronicle the actions of aristocratic characters. He might have chosen as his hero some nobleman with an inflated sense of honour, but then he probably could not have made him gullible enough to swallow Iago's lies. *And it is precisely the gullibility that is essential.* Shakespeare was not intent on emulating Heywood's achievement of the year before in *A Woman Killed With Kindness*. *Othello* is not a tragedy of jealousy: it is a tragedy of *groundless* jealousy.

So, in Cinthio's tale, Shakespeare found reconciled with a maximum of credibility the requirements of Renaissance tragedy and the necessities of his own private purpose: a character with a high rank in society, with a noble heart, and with an under-developed mind. It seems therefore reasonable to suppose that if Shakespeare was interested in Othello, it was not primarily because he is a barbarian, but because this noble savage provided him with a plausible example, suitable for use within the framework of the Renaissance view of tragedy, of a psychological characteristic that makes Othello the very antithesis of Hamlet. Othello's intellectual shortcomings have not passed unnoticed by students of the play, but the importance of this feature for its total meaning has not received the attention it deserves. We may say without exaggeration that Othello's lack of intellectual power is the basic element in his character. It is a necessary pre-requisite for his predicament. It is essential to the development of the situation as Shakespeare intended it to develop. And it may also throw some light on the nature of Shakespeare's tragic inspiration.

STEPS TO SELF-KNOWLEDGE

At the beginning of the play, Othello appears as a noble figure, generous, composed, self-possessed. Besides, he is glamorously happy, both as a general and as a husband. He seems to be a fully integrated man, a great personality at peace with itself. But if we care to scrutinize this impressive and attractive façade, we find that there is a crack in it, which might be described as follows: it is the happiness of a spoilt child, not of a mature mind; it is the brittle wholeness of innocence; it is pre-conscious, pre-rational, pre-moral. Othello has not yet come to grips with the experience of inner crisis. He has had to overcome no moral obstacles. He has not yet left the chamber of maiden-thought, and is still blessedly unaware of the burden of the mystery.

Of course, the life of a general, with its tradition of obedience and authority, is never likely to give rise to acute moral crises—especially at a time when war crimes had not yet been invented. But even Othello's love affair with Desdemona, judging by his own report, seems to have developed smoothly, without painful moral searchings of any kind. Nor is there for him any heart-rending contradiction between his love and his career: Desdemona is even willing to share the austerity of his flinty couch, so that he has every reason to believe that he will be allowed to make the best of both worlds.

Yet, at the core of this monolithic content, there is at least one ominous contradiction which announces the final disintegration of his personality: the contradiction between his obvious openheartedness, honesty and self-approval, and the fact that he does not think it beneath his dignity to court and marry Desdemona secretly. This contradiction is part and parcel of Shakespeare's conscious purpose. As Allardyce Nicoll has observed, there is no such secrecy in Cinthio's tale, where, instead, the marriage occurs openly, though in the teeth of fierce parental opposition.[9]

Highly significant, too, is the fact that he does not seem to feel any remorse for this most peculiar procedure. When at last he has to face the irate Brabantio, he gives no explanation, offers no apology for his conduct. Everything in his attitude shows that he is completely unaware of infringing the *mores* of Venetian society, the ethical code of Christian behaviour, and the sophisticated conventions of polite morality. Othello quietly thinks of himself as a civilized Christian and a prominent citizen of Venice, certainly not as a barbarian (see II, iii, 170–2). He shares in Desdemona's illusion that his true visage is in his mind.

Beside the deficient understanding of the society into which he has made his way, the motif of the secret marriage then also suggests a definite lack of self-knowledge on Othello's part. His first step towards "perception of sense" about himself occurs in the middle of Act III. While still trying to resist Iago's innuendoes, Othello exclaims:

> Excellent wretch! Perdition catch my soul,
> But I do love thee! and when I love thee not,
> Chaos is come again.   (III, iii, 90–2)

This word, "again", is perhaps the most unexpected word that Shakespeare could have used here. It is one of the most pregnant words in the whole tragedy. It indicates (a) Othello's dim sense that his life before he fell in love with Desdemona was in a state of chaos, in spite of the fact that he was at the time quite satisfied with it, and (b) his conviction that his love has redeemed him from chaos, has lifted him out of his former barbarousness. Such complacency shows his total obliviousness of the intricacies, the subtleties and the dangers of moral and spiritual growth. In this first anagnorisis, Othello realizes that he has lived so far in a sphere of spontaneous bravery and natural honesty, but he assumes without any further questionings that his love has gained him easy access to the sphere of moral awareness, of high spiritual existence.

In fact, he assumes that his super-ego has materialised, suddenly and without tears. Hence, of course, the impressive self-assurance of his demeanour in circumstances which would be most embarrassing to any man gifted with more accurate self-knowledge.

This first anagnorisis is soon followed by another one, in which Othello achieves some sort of recognition of what has become of him after his faith in Desdemona has been shattered. The short speech he utters then marks a new step forward in his progress to self-knowledge:

> I had been happy, if the general camp,
> Pioners and all, had tasted her sweet body,
> So I had nothing known. O, now, for ever
> Farewell the tranquil mind! farewell content!
> Farewell the plumed troop, and the big wars,
> That make ambition virtue! O, farewell!
> . . . .
> Farewell! Othello's occupation's gone!   (III, iii, 345-57)

The spontaneous outcry of the first three lines results from Othello's disturbed awareness that the new world he has entered into is one of (to him) unmanageable complexity. He is now facing a new kind of chaos, and he wishes he could take refuge in an ignorance similar to his former condition of moral innocence. The pathetic childishness of this ostrich-like attitude is proportionate in its intensity to the apparent monolithic quality of his previous complacency.

What follows sounds like a *non sequitur*. Instead of this farewell to arms, we might have expected some denunciation of the deceitful aspirations that have led him to this quandary, coupled, maybe, with a resolution to seek oblivion in renewed military activity. But we may surmise that his allusion to "the general camp", reminding him of his "occupation", turns his mind away from his immediate preoccupations. The transition occurs in the line

> Farewell the tranquil mind! farewell content!

which carries ambivalent implications. The content he has now lost is not only the "absolute content" his soul enjoyed as a result of his love for Desdemona: it is also the content he had known previously, at the time when he could rejoice in his "unhoused free condition". This was the content of innocence and spontaneous adjustment to life. There is no recovering it, for, in this respect, he reached a point of no return when he glimpsed the truly chaotic nature of that state of innocence.

The fact that Othello starts talking about himself in the third person is of considerable significance. G. R. Elliott has noticed that the words have "a piercing primitive appeal: he is now simply a name".[10] Besides, in this sudden ejaculation, there is a note of childish self-pity that reminds one of the first lines of the speech. But the main point is that it marks the occurrence of a deep dichotomy in Othello's consciousness of himself. As he had discarded his former self as an emblem of "chaos", so now he discards the super-ego that he thought had emerged into actual existence as a result of his love. It is as if that man known by the name of Othello was different from the one who will be speaking henceforward. The Othello of whom he speaks is the happy husband of Desdemona, the civilized Christian, the worthy Venetian, the illusory super-ego; but he is also the noble-spirited soldier and the natural man who guesses at heaven. That man has now disappeared, and the "I" who speaks of him is truly the savage Othello, the barbarian stripped of his wishful thinking, who gives himself up to jealousy, black magic and cruelty, the man who coarsely announces that he will "chop" his wife "into messes", the man who debases his magnificent oratory by borrowing shamelessly from Iago's lecherous vocabulary.

Thus Othello, whom love had brought from pre-rational, pre-moral satisfaction and adjustment to life to moral awareness and a higher form of "content", is now taken from excessive complacency and illusory happiness to equally excessive despair and nihilism. These are his steps to self-knowledge. That they should drive him to such alternative excesses gives the measure of his lack of judgment.

No Marriage of True Minds

From the purely psychological point of view of character-analysis, critics have always found it difficult satisfactorily to account for Othello's steep downfall. That it would have been easy, as Robert Bridges wrote, for Shakespeare "to have provided a more reasonable ground for Othello's jealousy", is obvious to all reasonable readers.[11] The fact that Othello's destruction occurs through the agency of Iago has induced the critics in the Romantic tradition to make much of what Coleridge has called Iago's "superhuman art", which, of course, relieves the Moor of all responsibility and deprives the play of most of its interest on the ethical and psychological level. More searching analyses, however, have shown that Iago is far from being a devil in disguise.[12] And T. S. Eliot has exposed the Moor as a case of *bovarysme*, or "the human will to see things as they are not",[13] while Leo Kirschbaum has denounced him as "a romantic idealist, who considers human nature superior to what it actually is".[14]

For our examination of *Othello* as a study in the relationships between the intellect and the moral life, it is interesting to note that the ultimate responsibility for the fateful development of the plot rests with a flaw in Othello himself. There is no "reasonable ground" for his jealousy; or, to put it somewhat differently, Shakespeare did not chose to provide any "reasonable" ground for it. The true motive, we may safely deduce, must be unreasonable. Yet, I find it difficult to agree that the Moor "considers human nature superior to what it actually is": this may be true of his opinion of Iago, but Desdemona is really the emblem of purity and trustworthiness that he initially thought her to be. Nor can we justifiably speak of his "*will* to see things as they are not" (though these words might actually fit Desdemona); in his confusion and perplexity there is no opportunity for his will to exert itself in any direction. The basic element that permits Othello's destiny to evolve the way it does is his utter *inability* to grasp the actual. If we want to locate with any accuracy the psychological origin of what F. R. Leavis has called his "readiness to respond" to Iago's fiendish suggestions, we cannot escape the conclusion that his gullibility makes manifest his lack of rationality, of psychological insight and of mere common sense, and that it is a necessary product of his undeveloped mind.

Othello has to choose between trusting Iago and trusting Desdemona. This is the heart of the matter, put in the simplest possible terms. The question, then, is: why does he rate Iago's honesty higher than Desdemona's? If it is admitted that Iago is not a symbol of devilish skill in evil-doing, but a mere fallible villain, the true answer can only be that Othello does not know his own wife.

17

More than a century of sentimental criticism based on the Romantic view of Othello as the trustful, chivalrous and sublime lover, has blurred our perception of his feeling for Desdemona. The quality of his "love" has recently been gone into with unprecedented thoroughness by G. R. Elliott, who points out that the Moor's speech to the Duke and Senators (I, iii) shows that "his affection for her, though fixed and true, is comparatively superficial".[15] Othello sounds, indeed, curiously detached about Desdemona. His love is clearly subordinated, at that moment, to his soldierly pride. If he asks the Duke to let her go to Cyprus with him, it is because *she* wants it, it is "to be free and bounteous to her mind". In the juxtaposition of Desdemona's and Othello's speeches about this, there is an uncomfortable suggestion that his love is not at all equal to hers, who "did love the Moor to live with him", and that he is not interested in her as we feel he ought to be. At a later stage the same self-centredness colours his vision of Desdemona as the vital source of his soul's life and happiness: his main concern lies with the "joy" (II, i, 186), the "absolute content" (II, i, 193), the salvation (III, iii, 90–1) of his own soul, not with Desdemona as a woman in love, a human person. It lies with *his* love and the changes his love has wrought in him, rather than with the object of his love. It is not surprising, then, that he should know so little about his wife's inner life as to believe the charges raised by Iago.

On the other hand, his attitude to Desdemona is truly one of idealization, but in a very limited, one might even say philosophical, sense. Coleridge wrote that "Othello does not kill Desdemona in jealousy, but in the belief that she, his angel, had fallen from the heaven of her native innocence".[16] But Coleridge failed to stress the most important point, which is that this belief is mistaken. Desdemona is *not* "impure and worthless", she has *not* fallen from the heaven of her native innocence. Othello is unable to recognize this, and his failure is thus primarily an intellectual failure.

His attitude to Desdemona is different from that of the "romantic idealist" who endows his girl with qualities which she does not possess. Desdemona does have all the qualities that her husband expects to find in her. What matters to him, however, is not Desdemona as she is, but Desdemona as a symbol, or, in other words, it is his vision of Desdemona.

In his *Essay on Man*, Ernst Cassirer has the following remark about the working of the primitive mind:

In primitive thought, it is still very difficult to differentiate between the two spheres of being and meaning. They are constantly being confused: a symbol is looked upon as if it were endowed with magical or metaphysical powers.[17]

That is just what has happened to Othello: in Desdemona he has failed to differentiate between the human being and the angelic symbol. Or rather, he has overlooked the woman in his preoccupation with the angel. She is to him merely the emblem of his highest ideal, and their marriage is merely the ritual of his admission into her native world, into her spiritual sphere of values. Because he is identifying "the two spheres of being and meaning", he is possessed by the feeling that neither these values nor his accession to them have any actual existence outside her: his lack of psychological insight is only matched by his lack of rational power.

The Neo-Platonic conceit that the lover's heart and soul have their dwelling in the person of the beloved is used by Othello in a poignantly literal sense (IV, ii, 57–60). If she fails him, everything fails him. If she is not pure, then purity does not exist. If she is not true to his ideal, that means that his ideal is an illusion. If it can be established that she does not belong to that world in which he sees her enshrined, that means that there is no such world. She becomes completely and explicitly identified with all higher spiritual values when he says:

> If she be false, O! then heaven mocks itself! (III, iii, 278)

Hence the apocalyptic quality of his nihilism and despair.

The fundamental tragic fault in the Moor can therefore be said to lie in the shortcomings of his intellect. His moral balance is without any rational foundation. He is entirely devoid of the capacity for abstraction. He fails to make the right distinction between the sphere of meaning, of the abstract, the ideal, the universal, and the sphere of being, of the concrete, the actual, the singular.

When Othello is finally made to see the truth, he recognizes the utter lack of wisdom (v, ii, 344) which is the mainspring of his tragedy, and, in the final anagnorisis, he sees himself for what he is: a "fool" (v, ii, 323). The full import of the story is made clear in Othello's last speech, which is so seldom given the attention it merits that it may be well to quote it at some length:

> I pray you, in your letters,
> When you shall these unlucky deeds relate,
> Speak of me as I am; nothing extenuate,
> Nor set down aught in malice: then, must you speak
> Of one that loved not wisely but too well;
> Of one not easily jealous, but being wrought
> Perplex'd in the extreme; of one whose hand,
> Like the base Indian, threw a pearl away
> Richer than all his tribe; of one whose subdued eyes,
> Albeit unused to the melting mood,
> Drop tears as fast as the Arabian trees
> Their medicinal gum. Set you down this;
> And say besides, that in Aleppo once,
> Where a malignant and a turban'd Turk
> Beat a Venetian and traduced the state,
> I took by the throat the circumcised dog,
> And smote him, thus. (*Stabs himself*) (v, ii, 340–56)

One may find it strange that Shakespeare should have introduced at the end of Othello's last speech this apparently irrelevant allusion to a trivial incident in the course of which the Moor killed a Turk who had insulted Venice. But if we care to investigate the allegorical potentialities of the speech, we find that it is not a mere fit of oratorical self-dramatization: it clarifies the meaning of the play as a whole. There is a link between the pearl, the Venetian and Desdemona: taken together, they are an emblem of beauty, moral virtue, spiritual richness and civilized refinement. And there is a link between the "base Indian", the "malignant Turk" and Othello himself: all three are barbarians: all three have shown themselves unaware of the true value and dignity of what lay within their reach. Othello has thrown his pearl away, like the Indian. In so doing, he has insulted, like the Turk, everything that Venice and Desdemona stand for. As the Turk "traduced the State", so did Othello misrepresent to himself that heaven of which Desdemona was the sensuous image.

S. L. Bethell has left us in no doubt that the manner of Othello's death was intended by Shakespeare as an indication that the hero is doomed to eternal damnation.[18] Such a view provides us with a suitable climax for this tragedy. Othello has attained full consciousness of his barbarian nature; yet, even that ultimate flash of awareness does not lift him up above his true self. He remains a barbarian to the very end, and condemns his own soul to the everlasting torments of hell in obeying the same primitive sense of rough-handed justice that had formerly prompted him to kill Desdemona: it is a natural culmination to what a Swiss critic has aptly called "eine Tragödie der Verirrung".[19]

NOTES

1. G. Wilson Knight, 'The *Othello* Music' in *The Wheel of Fire* (1930; fourth edition, 1949). J. I. M. Stewart, *Character and Motive in Shakespeare* (1949).

2. For a close discussion of the views of Rymer, Bridges and Stoll, cf. Stewart, *op. cit.*

3. T. S. Eliot, 'Shakespeare and the Stoicism of Seneca', in *Selected Essays* (1932); G. R. Elliott, *Flaming Minister. A Study of Othello* (Duke University Press, Durham, 1953).

4. R. S. Crane, *The Languages of Criticism and the Structure of Poetry* (Toronto, 1953), p. 147. The quotations are taken from a discussion of R. B. Heilman's method in his 'More Fair than Black: Light and Dark in *Othello*', *Essays in Criticism*, I (1951), 315–35.

5. H. B. Charlton, 'Othello', in *Shakespearian Tragedy* (Cambridge, 1948).

6. Cf. Coleridge, *Lectures and Notes on Shakespere and Other English Poets* (1904), p. 386.

7. Levin L. Schucking, in *Shakespeare und der Tragödienstil seiner Zeit* (Bern, 1947) considers Othello's belief in Iago's honesty as "eine der Hauptschwächen in der Konstruction der Fabel", for, he says "es ist höchst unwahrscheinlich, dasz Othello nach so langem Zusammenleben im Kriegsdienst sich derart über den bösartigen Character seines Fahnrichs im unklaren geblieben sein sollte" (p. 68). The general consensus about Iago's honesty, carefully stressed by Shakespeare, should nullify this particular criticism.

8. Mark Van Doren, *Shakespeare* (New York, 1953), p. 196.

9. Allardyce Nicoll, *Shakespeare* (1952), p. 144.

10. G. R. Elliott, *op. cit.* p. 130, n. 30.

11. R. Bridges, 'The Influence of the Audience on Shakespeare's Drama' in *Collected Essays*, I (1927).

12. Cf. G. R. Elliott, *op. cit. passim*; J. I. M. Stewart, *op. cit.* p. 103; and F. R. Leavis, 'Diabolic Intellect and the Noble Hero', in *The Common Pursuit* (1952), p. 140.

13. T. S. Eliot, *op. cit.*

14. In *ELH*, December 1944 (quoted by J. I. M. Stewart, *op. cit.* p. 104).

15. G. R. Elliott, *op. cit.* p. 34.

16. Coleridge, *op. cit.* pp. 393 and 529.

17. E. Cassirer, *An Essay on Man* (New Haven, 1944), p. 57.

18. S. L. Bethell, 'Shakespeare's Imagery: The Diabolic Images in *Othello*', pp. 29–47 of this volume.

19. R. Fricker, *Kontrast und Polarität in den Charakterbildern Shakespeares* (Bern, 1951).

EXTRACT FROM THE INDIVIDUALIZATION OF SHAKESPEARE'S CHARACTERS THROUGH IMAGERY

BY

MIKHAIL M. MOROZOV

The degree to which and the means by which Shakespeare individualized the style of speech used by his various characters are still unsettled.[1] This question is of practical as well as theoretical interest—especially for actors of Shakespearian roles and for translators of Shakespeare. This is particularly true of the Soviet theatre which, as I have noted elsewhere,[2] strives for the maximum individualization of Shakespeare's characters.

Rowe, Shakespeare's first biographer (1709), and Alexander Pope maintained that even if Shakespeare had not indicated the names of the characters speaking in the text, we would have been able to recognize them. Although the great dramatist's English has since been covered with "the dust of ages", many modern readers 'instinctively' feel that Hamlet, for instance, speaks differently from Ophelia, that Othello's style of speech is different from Iago's. Wherein, exactly, does this difference lie? Strange as it may seem, this question has not been thoroughly studied to this day.

Shakespeare's language, as everyone knows, is exceptionally rich in imagery. "Every word with him is a picture", Thomas Gray wrote of Shakespeare. This suggests the hypothesis that the 'natures' of the characters may in some measure be reflected in these pictures. In real life, in our every-day speech, we quite probably usually compare the things we talk about with that which is particularly near and comprehensible to each of us. In literature the case is evidently often different, for in inventing a metaphor the poet or writer may disregard his personal inclinations in favour of the aesthetic canons of some definite 'school' or 'tradition'. In plays the characters frequently speak in the language, and hence the images, of the author. Hypotheses alone, like 'instinctive' feelings, are far from sufficient.

In discussing the distinctively individual features of Shakespeare's characters in his book *Shakespeare's Language and Style*,[3] the author of these lines wrote: "The range of the predominating image met with in the speeches of a character is of tremendous significance." This assertion, however, was not bolstered up at that time by an analysis of the facts. Most probably, in the vast literature on Shakespeare, quite a number of such similar assertions are to be found. However, there is a no lesser abundance of denials of any definitely defined individuality in the speech styles of his characters. True, the overwhelming majority of books on Shakespeare do not touch on this question at all, although it is of paramount importance to a study of Shakespeare's poetics.

The most fundamental investigation of Shakespeare's imagery is Caroline Spurgeon's well-known book *Shakespeare's Imagery*.[4] In this book, however, his imagery is considered only in respect to all his work as a whole, or in respect to some one play. Spurgeon does not touch on the part imagery plays in revealing character. Only in the appendix of her book does she make any mention of the other interesting functions of imagery. Listing these functions, she speaks of the assistance a study of imagery can be in revealing the temperament and nature of the character who uses this imagery. This is a very interesting theme, she says, and is worth investigating. To prove her point she cites Falstaff's imagery in the two parts of *Henry IV* as offering clear indication of the change which takes place in the stout knight.[5]

Spurgeon touched on this rich theme only briefly and in passing. As we have already said, most Shakespeare studies do not deal with this theme at all, while many of them deny or minimize the distinct individuality of the style of speech used by each of Shakespeare's characters.

About twenty years ago, thanks to the studies of Dover Wilson and Granville-Barker,[6] it was the fashion among English students of Shakespeare to regard Shakespeare chiefly as a dramatist. Of recent years, however, Shakespeare is coming more and more to be regarded chiefly as a 'dramatic poet'. The realism of Shakespeare's characters, their specific psychological traits, and hence distinctive styles of speech, are often being thrown into obscurity.[7]

We are obliged to erect the edifice of our investigation on an unexplored site. If, as a result of our investigation, we should find definite laws governing the imagery of the individual characters we shall thereby, first, again confirm the fact that Shakespeare's characters do not speak for the author but, so to say, 'for themselves', i.e. are independent individuals (in other words we shall obtain new confirmation of Shakespeare's *realism*); secondly, we shall record *one* of the means by which Shakespeare (probably subconsciously) individualized the speech of his characters; and, finally, the particular figures of speech predominating in the role of any given character will provide us with a valuable key to that character's psychological make-up.

1. *OTHELLO*

OTHELLO

The images to be found in Othello's speeches fall into two sharply contrasting groups. First—and chiefly—there is what may be called *lofty* and *poetic* imagery. Instead of saying "for the greatest fortune" Othello says "for the sea's worth" (I, ii, 28). He says that Desdemona "was false as water" (V, ii, 132). Instead of "always be suspecting" Othello says "to follow still the changes of the moon with fresh suspicions" (III, iii, 178).

It is a noteworthy fact that the image of the moon occurs four more times in Othello's speeches: instead of "nine months" he has "nine moons" (I, iii, 84); "the moon winks" (IV, ii, 76) to hide Desdemona's supposed adultery from its eyes; after murdering Desdemona Othello compares the catastrophe to "a huge eclipse of sun and moon" (V, ii, 99) and states that the moon "makes men mad" (V, ii, 107). In this repetition of the word 'moon' we divine something peculiar to the man, something of Oriental origin, the 'atmosphere' Pushkin felt:

> Why does young Desdemona
> Love her Moor
> As the moon loves the dark of night....

This first impression is confirmed by others of Othello's florid and grandiose figures of speech. He does not say that the sybil who sewed the handkerchief he presented to Desdemona was two hundred years old, but that she "had number'd in the world the sun to course two hundred compasses" (III, iv, 72). He invokes the "chaste stars" (v, ii, 2). To kill Desdemona means "to put out the light" (v, ii, 7). The lamp he holds in his hand is a "flaming minister" (v, ii, 8). To kill Desdemona is to pluck the rose (v, ii, 13), to kiss her as she sleeps is to smell the rose on the tree (v, ii, 18). Had Desdemona been true to him he would not have sold her for a world made "of one entire and perfect chrysolite" (v, ii, 143). Desdemona's skin is whiter "than snow, and smooth as monumental alabaster" (v, ii, 4). Instead of saying that he is a man already advanced in years, Othello says that he is "declined into the vale of years" (III, iii, 266). He compares Desdemona to a hawk (III, iii, 265) and to the fountain from which his current runs (IV, ii, 58). Instead of simply vowing "by heaven", he says much more picturesquely "by yond marble heaven", with marble probably used as a synonym for enduring, constant, inviolable. He calls patience a "young and rose-lipt cherubin" (IV, ii, 62). Learning, after her death, that Desdemona was innocent, Othello weeps tears of joy and compares his tears with the "medicinable gum" of "the Arabian trees" (v, ii, 349). After Desdemona's death he compares himself with "the base Indian", who "threw a pearl away richer than all his tribe" (v, ii, 346). Contemplating death he speaks of the "very sea-mark of my utmost sail" (v, ii, 267). The following images, too, it seems, should be classed as poetic. Othello compares his heart to a stone: he strikes his breast and it hurts his hand (IV, i, 181). The image of a heart turned to stone recurs in Othello's speeches: "thou dost stone my heart", he tells Desdemona (v, ii, 63). Othello tells the Senators that custom "hath made the flinty and steel couch of war my thrice-driven bed of down" (I, iii, 231).

Thus, lofty and poetic images are abundant in Othello's speech. The epithet *poetic* is particularly appropriate to them. Some of them are full of Oriental atmosphere: the moon, the "two hundred compasses" of the sun, the fragrance of roses, a world of chrysolite, skin as white as alabaster. The gum of Arabian trees and the Indian with his pearl are frankly exotic. Investigators who refuse to admit exotic colour in Othello's role are therefore in the wrong.

The numerous classical images he uses are also of the lofty and poetic type. He speaks, for instance, of the "light-wing'd toys of feather'd Cupid" (I, iii, 268). Waves are "hills of seas Olympus-high" (II, i, 191). Thunder is "th' Immortal Jove's dread clamours" (III, iii, 356). Desdemona's name was, according to Othello, "as fresh as Dian's visage" (III, iii, 388). He compares his feelings with the Pontic (Black) sea which flows ever forward (III, iii, 453). He calls life "Promethean heat" (v, ii, 12). The image of chaos in the famous phrase "when I love thee not, Chaos is come again" (III, iii, 92) is also to be regarded as classical. Finally, the image of a personified justice evoked by the words: "O balmy breath, that dost almost persuade Justice to break her sword" (v, ii, 16), may also be included here. Justice is allegorically pictured as a feminine figure carrying a sword.

Lofty, poetic and solemn imagery is so abundant and so essential in Othello's role that we are quite justified in calling it the dominant theme in his world of images. However, it is not the only theme. In sharp contrast to it there is another theme represented by a whole group of images which may be called low.

Othello calls a suspicious, jealous man a 'goat' (III, iii, 180). "Goats and monkeys!" he exclaims in a fit of jealousy (IV, i, 264).[8] He says he "had rather be a toad, and live upon the vapour of a dungeon" than be cuckolded (III, iii, 270). He compares Desdemona to "a cistern for foul toads to knot and gender in" (IV, ii, 60). He commands his bosom to swell with its "fraught, for 'tis of aspics' tongues" (III, iii, 451). Desdemona's singing, he says, is capable of taming a bear, thereby comparing himself with a savage bear (IV, i, 188). "If that the earth could teem with woman's tears, each drop she [Desdemona] falls would prove a crocodile" he says (IV, i, 256). He declares that Desdemona is 'honest' as "summer flies are in the shambles that quicken even with blowing" (IV, ii, 65). He calls the infidelity of wives a "forked plague" (III, iii, 276). It is remarkable that this theme—the theme of the menagerie—goats, monkeys, toads, aspics, wild bears, crocodiles, flies—is absolutely identical, as we shall see, with the dominant theme of Iago's imagery.

Othello's famous comparison of his thoughts about Desdemona's handkerchief with a raven over an infected house (IV, i, 20) is pervaded with bleak gloom. And his comparison of Desdemona herself with a lovely, fair, sweet-smelling weed (IV, ii, 66) is an image in which, side by side with its poetic quality, there is something akin to Iago's dominant theme.

Othello says that Iago has "set me on the rack" (III, iii, 336). He compares his cheeks, ready to burn with shame, with a forge (IV, ii, 73). He says that had all Cassio's hairs "been lives, my great revenge had stomach for them all" (V, ii, 75).

The image of a monster appears twice in Othello's speeches. He says of Iago "there were some monster in his thought too hideous to be shown" (III, iii, 106). "A horned man's a monster and a beast", he declares (IV, i, 62). As we shall see the image of jealousy as a monster recurs in the speeches of Iago, Desdemona and Emilia.

Thus, besides the lofty, poetic and bright images, which predominate in Othello's world of images, we also find mean images (goats, monkeys, toads, etc.) and gloomy images which sometimes have a suggestion of the demonic (the raven over an infected house). This contrast is strikingly conveyed in one of Othello's images: "And let the labouring bark climb hills of seas Olympus-high, and duck again as low as hell's from heaven" (II, i, 190). The first, poetic, theme is properly Othello's; the second, low, theme is, as we shall see later, borrowed.

It is noteworthy that the low and gloomy images are not scattered haphazardly through Othello's speeches. They invade his speeches, violating the bright dominant theme, at a logical point—following the words "and when I love thee not, Chaos is come again" (III, iii, 92). This is the point at which Iago gains the ascendancy over Othello's soul, so that the latter begins to think in Iago's images, to see the world with Iago's eyes.

It is also a fact worthy of note that Othello returns to his own dominant theme not after he learns of Desdemona's innocence, but much earlier. In the scene of Desdemona's death there is only one low and coarse image: Othello says that had all Cassio's hairs been lives, his great revenge had had stomach for them all (V, ii, 75). This is merely a reflection, a reminiscence of a past mood, as is the coarse word 'whore' which escapes him twice in this same scene. On the whole, Othello's part in the scene of Desdemona's death abounds in lofty and poetic imagery. The monologue he pronounces over the sleeping Desdemona at the beginning of the second scene of Act V is particularly rich in such imagery, for Othello kills Desdemona loving her.

In his monologue in Act III, Scene 3, Othello speaks of "plumed troops", of the "spirit-stirring drum", of the "royal banner", of the "rude throats" of "mortal engines", etc. For the rest there are no military motifs in Othello's imagery, with the exception, perhaps, that, when meeting Desdemona at Cyprus, he calls her "my fair warrior" (II, i, 185). It is interesting to note that his classical images likewise do not deal with military motifs: neither Mars nor Caesar is mentioned.

We shall not touch on the scattered, incidental images in Othello's speech which do not constitute integral groups. For instance, early in the play we meet a metaphor very typical of Shakespeare in general, a metaphor of the theatre. "Were it my cue to fight, I should have known it without a prompter" (I, ii, 82). Or, to take another example, there is an image from Biblical legend. Othello says that Emilia has an office opposite to that of Saint Peter; i.e. that she keeps the gates of hell (IV, ii, 90). All these scattered themes are not of importance to us.

Thus we find a definite order in Othello's world of images. The lofty-poetic dominant is over-powered by the low theme stemming from Iago, only to triumph again at the last. The point at which the second theme makes its invasion is the image: "Chaos is come again." It is our opinion that this image has an objective rather than a subjective meaning, i.e. that chaos has come again in the universe, that the cosmos, the universe, has been upset; in other words, that the world has changed in Othello's eyes. Were we to take this image as subjective, i.e. as meaning that chaos had returned to Othello's soul, we should have to assume that chaos had already been resident there at some former time, an assumption for which there are no grounds in the text. Othello's story of his life (his monologue in the Senate) confirms that the lofty-poetic theme, connected with the cosmos, is 'native' to Othello, that he is a highly *harmonic* man and that, consequently, the low theme, connected with chaos, comes wholly from Iago.

IAGO

The low images prove predominant in Iago's role. The prevailing images are of beasts, represented as embodiments of foolishness, lechery and all kinds of loathsome vices. Iago sees the surrounding world as a stable or malodorous menagerie. A faithful servant is like an ass (I, i, 46). Othello is trustful and can be led by the nose like an ass (I, iii, 407). Iago says that Othello will yet reward him for making him an ass (II, i, 321). He does not want to "wear my heart upon my sleeve for daws to peck at" (I, i, 64). "Plague him [Othello] with flies", i.e. with petty annoyances, Iago counsels Roderigo (I, i, 71). Othello is "an old black ram" tupping a "white ewe" (I, i, 88). The carousing warriors of Cyprus are a "*flock* of drunkards" (II, iii, 62). Othello is "a Barbary horse", Brabantio's grandchildren will neigh, and Brabantio will have coursers and gennets for relatives (I, i, 112 f.). When in each other's arms, Othello and Desdemona make "the beast with two backs" (I, i, 117). Iago calls Desdemona a prostitute, choosing the jargon word 'guinea-hen' as a synonym; he dissuades Roderigo from drowning himself for love of a 'guinea-hen' (I, iii, 318). He says that sooner than do that he would "change my humanity with a baboon" (I, iii, 319). "Drown cats and blind puppies", he tells Roderigo (I, iii, 341). Women in their kitchens are 'wild-cats' (II, i, 110). In Iago's words one man differs from another as "the cod's head" from "the salmon's tail" (II, i, 155). "With as little a web as this will I ensnare as great a fly as Cassio" (II, i, 169) says Iago, comparing himself to a spider. He compares Roderigo to a hunting dog which he sets upon Cassio (II, i, 316). When Cassio has drunk some wine, he will become as quarrelsome as Desdemona's dog (II, iii, 54). He assures Cassio that Othello has punished him for the sake of policy, in order to put fear into the hearts of the people of Cyprus, "as one would beat his offenceless dog to affright an imperious lion" (II, iii, 278). Cassio and Desdemona are, in his words, as lecherous as goats, monkeys and wolves (III, iii, 404). He compares a married man to a yoked ox (IV, i, 67). This 'menagerie' of Iago's is reflected, as we have seen, in Othello's speeches, forming the second theme (goats, monkeys, toads) in the latter's world of images. Iago does indeed succeed in poisoning Othello's soul for a time.

Other low images fit in with the 'menagerie'. "The food", says Iago, "that to him now is as luscious as locusts shall be to him shortly as bitter as coloquintida" (I, iii, 354). Iago compares Cassio's slender fingers to 'clysterpipes' (II, i, 179). When Roderigo speaks of Desdemona's "blest condition", Iago mocks him, saying "blest fig's end" (II, i, 260). He calls Roderigo a "young quat" he has rubbed "almost to the sense" (v, i, 11).

His images are generally concrete and substantial. He compares the human body with a garden, will with gardeners: what we plant in this garden depends upon ourselves. Idleness he compares with sterility, industry with manure, love is the scion of lust (I, iii, 324 f.). "My invention", he says of himself, "comes from my pate as birdlime does from frize" (II, i, 126). He calls Cassio, the military theoretician, a 'counter-caster' (I, i, 31). In his opinion Cassio understands no "more than a spinster" in the tactics of battle (I, i, 24). He ironically calls his slander 'medicine': "Work on, my medicine, work!" (IV, i, 46). The suspicion that Othello has lived with Emilia gnaws his vitals "like a poisonous mineral" (II, i, 309). "Dangerous conceits", he reflects, "are, in their natures, poisons" (III, iii, 326).

Iago frequently repeats the word 'devil'. Usually he employs it merely as a swear word. He calls black Othello a 'devil' (I, i, 91). "You are one of those", he tells Brabantio, "that will not serve God, if the devil bid you" (I, i, 109). Offended women, Iago says, are 'devils' in their anger (II, i, 111).

However, besides this form of swearing, Iago's imagery also contains demonic motifs. "Hell and night", he says, "must bring this monstrous birth to the world's light" (I, iii, 409). "I do hate him [Othello] as I do hell-pains", says Iago (I, i, 155). "There are many events", he declares, "in the womb of time, which will be deliver'd" (I, iii, 378). The following image also has a suggestion of the demonic. In the scene before Brabantio's house Iago tells Roderigo to shout "with like timorous accent and dire yell as when by night and negligence, the fire is spied in populous cities" (I, i, 76). The demonic motif in Iago's role receives its most striking expression in the image of jealousy as a monster, an image we have already met in Othello's role. Iago, however, gives fuller expression to this image. He calls jealousy "the green-eyed monster which doth mock the meat it feeds on" (III, iii, 166).

Lofty-poetic images, which, as we have seen, constitute the dominant theme in Othello's imagery, are totally lacking in Iago's role. True, in a dialogue with Othello, he calls a good name "the immediate jewel" of the soul (III, iii, 156), but he is here obviously imitating Othello's 'style'. He also says that Desdemona has been "framed as fruitful as the free elements" (II, iii, 350), and terms the soldiers of Cyprus "the very elements of this warlike isle" (II, iii, 60). If these are exceptions, they prove the rule. It is much more likely that we are here dealing with *exclusions*. We introduce this term to denote those passages in Shakespeare where a character seems to exclude himself (switch over) from his proper role and assume the function of a chorus, explaining the events taking place, describing other characters, etc., quite regardless of his own individuality. It is common knowledge that such passages are to be found quite frequently in Shakespeare. In any case, whether this is exception or 'exclusion', we have, on the whole, every right to say that Iago's role is devoid of lofty-poetic imagery.

We do find a few classical images in his speeches. He swears by Janus (I, ii, 33). It is characteristic, by the way, that he swears by a two-faced God! He says that Cassio's military abilities are such as make him fit to stand with Caesar (II, iii, 128). He tells Cassio that Desdemona would have been "sport for Jove" (II, iii, 17). In contrast to the peaceful classical images in Othello's role (Cupid, Diana) Iago's are of a warlike nature (Janus, the god of war, and Caesar). Iago is a professional soldier, a soldier by trade, and it is therefore not to be wondered at that he himself speaks of "the trade of War" (I, ii, 1).

There is one other group of images in Iago's role which is evidently not accidental, for it is quite a large and distinct group. These are typically naval images. Iago says that Cassio "be-lee'd and calm'd" him, i.e. won promotion over his head (I, i, 30). Instead of saying that the Senate had no other man of such abilities as Othello, as we would say to-day, Iago says that "another of his fathom they have none" (I, i, 153).

Iago says that he must put out "a flag and sign of love, which is indeed but sign" (I, i, 157). Brabantio, in Iago's words, will pursue Othello, in so far as "the law...will give him cable" (I, ii, 17). Iago assures Roderigo that he is knit to him with "cables of perdurable toughness" (I, iii, 343). Iago expresses it that in marrying Desdemona Othello "hath boarded a land carack" (I, ii, 50), which in sailor's slang of that time meant a prostitute. Iago doubts whether it will prove a "lawful prize", an expression typical of freebooters. "My boat sails freely, both with wind and stream", says Iago (II, iii, 66). All this seems to indicate that Iago was probably once a sailor. In any case, he had been in England (II, iii, 79), and had also observed Danes, Germans and Hollanders drinking themselves drunk.

DESDEMONA

Desdemona's role is poor in imagery, but whatever there is of it is characteristic. First there are poetic motifs: Desdemona accompanies her husband to the wars because she does not want to sit at home and be "a moth of peace" (I, iii, 258). She sings about the willow tree (IV, iii, 41), privately comparing herself to it, for the willow used to be the symbol of a girl or woman abandoned by her lover (Ophelia drowns under a weeping willow). "Her salt tears fell from her", sings Desdemona, "and soften'd the stones" (IV, iii, 47)—an image echoing the image of the stony heart which occurs twice in Othello's role. Desdemona cannot understand why Othello should have changed toward her and says that evidently something "hath puddled his clear spirit" (III, iv, 142), and this, too, echoes Othello's expression, cited above, that Desdemona is his 'fountain'. Desdemona's statement that "I'll watch him tame" (III, iii, 23) implies a comparison of Othello to a hawk, and these words again echo Othello, who, as we have seen, likens Desdemona to a hawk. Thus, many of the images used by Desdemona echo Othello's images.

Desdemona's role also includes images of everyday domestic things. She says that she will tirelessly persuade Othello to reinstate Cassio: "His bed shall seem a school, his board a shrift" (III, iii, 24). She says that her request to reinstate Cassio is as if she were asking Othello to "wear gloves, or feed on nourishing dishes, or keep you warm" (III, iii, 77). The following is closely related to the same group of domestic, intimate images: when a finger aches all the other members of the body seem to share the pain (III, iv, 145).

There is also a militant-heroic note in Desdemona's imagery. "That I did love the Moor to live with him, My downright violence and storm of fortunes May trumpet to the world!" she declares in the Senate (I, iii, 250). Paraphrasing Othello, who called her a "fair warrior", she calls herself an "unhandsome warrior" (III, iv, 150).

Finally, in Desdemona's speeches, as in Othello's, Iago's and Emilia's, there occurs the image of jealousy as a monster. When Emilia calls jealousy a monster "begot upon itself, born on itself", Desdemona exclaims: "Heaven keep that monster from Othello's mind!" (III, iv, 162).

The combination of poetic with domestic images, the presence of a militant, heroic note, and echoes or reflections of the images used by Othello who rules her being—this is the world of Desdemona's imagery.

Thus, we have found that each of the three leading characters in this tragedy has his own world of images. This is, of course, much more strikingly and sharply evident in the roles of Othello and Iago. Desdemona's images are much paler.

NOTES

1. The present paper is a fragment of an investigation of Shakespeare's poetics.
2. Cf. "Shakespeare on the Soviet Stage", *Theatre Almanac* (All-Union Theatre Society, no. 6, 1947).
3. Cf. *From the History of English Realism* (U.S.S.R. Academy of Sciences Press, 1941).
4. Caroline F. E. Spurgeon, *Shakespeare's Imagery* (Cambridge, 1935).
5. Spurgeon, *ibid.* pp. 379–80.
6. Cf. Dover Wilson, *What Happens in Hamlet* (Cambridge, 1937); Granville-Barker, *Prefaces to Shakespeare* (1927).
7. For instance, see Bethell, *Shakespeare and the Popular Dramatic Tradition* (1944).
8. The usual interpretation: Othello recalls Iago's words, comparing Cassio and Desdemona to lecherous goats and monkeys. But N. Mordvinov in the role of Othello (as produced by Yuri Zavadsky in the Mossoviet Theatre in Moscow, 1942) addressed the words to all the characters present on the stage: at that moment the whole world seemed to Othello to be a menagerie. As the reader sees, both interpretations are possible: all people begin to seem beasts to Othello; on the other hand, this is the result of Iago's influence, an echo of his theme.

SHAKESPEARE'S IMAGERY: THE DIABOLIC IMAGES IN *OTHELLO*

BY

S. L. BETHELL

There is still no commonly accepted procedure in Shakespeare criticism. Yet method to a great extent determines results. Unfortunately no one to-day can have a specialist's familiarity with every department of Shakespeare studies: indeed, it is arguable that the talents of the critic and those required by the modern textual scholar are seldom to be found in the same person. The critic is usually willing to defer to specialist authority on textual and bibliographical questions, but other departments of scholarship, notably the study of Elizabethan thought and Elizabethan theatrical conditions, are indispensable. Without these safeguards the approach to Shakespeare's imagery is especially perilous.

I. METHOD

The study of poetic imagery is without doubt one of the most important innovations in Shakespeare criticism, but, unless a method is followed which brings imagery into due sub-ordination to other aspects of dramatic expression, it can lead only to the construction of individual fantasies. There would seem to have been hitherto a good deal of confusion about the nature and function of Shakespeare's imagery and about the critical technique required to deal with it. It might be useful to examine some of the more important problems involved.

(*a*) There is a matter of definition. The late Caroline Spurgeon used 'imagery' in a strict sense: her elaborate tabulations refer only to such images as occur in rhetorical figures, metaphor and so forth. But direct reference is poetically as important as the oblique reference of a figure, and, moreover, since there is less likelihood of its being unconscious, it is more likely to be directly relevant to the main theme. In what follows I shall widen the scope of the term 'image' to cover any reference in word or phrase to a distinct object or class of objects, whether used figuratively or directly.

(*b*) There is also the problem of interpretation. Three methods are employed by different types of critic. (i) For the psycho-analyst, images stand for realities of the Unconscious very different from their apparent significance. Psycho-analytic criticism, however, can have little interest for those who do not accept the system of belief on which it depends. It is not just another tool, made generally available by the activity of a body of specialists; it has no validity outside the context of a particular group of psychological theories. (ii) Interpreters such as Wilson Knight are concerned with what the images mean to us, to the modern reader, apart from historical limitations, while (iii) a more recent group of scholars, mainly American, are engaged in discovering what they meant to the Elizabethans. Method (ii) seems to assume that Shakespeare's use of imagery was largely unconscious (i.e. indeliberate, a different connotation from the 'Unconscious' of Method (i)), that he habitually expressed profounder meanings than he was consciously aware of. Method (iii) stresses the learned and deliberate artist, employing his figures according to precept and with full awareness of their philosophical and other implications. The latter view is probably nearer to the truth, though we must also recognize that all poetry has an unconscious element which becomes clear only when a particular work is considered in relation to the wider framework of poetic tradition. It seems that Methods (ii) and (iii) might benefit from cross-fertilization. With Method (ii) there is a danger of 'reading in' to Shakespeare a modern—and perhaps a personal—set of attitudes and concerns; the danger of Method (iii) is that, in a purely scholarly application of Elizabethan poetic theory and philosophy, Shakespeare might be reduced to merely a typical Elizabethan. The two methods together are necessary if we are both to understand what Shakespeare was really doing and also to give him his place in a living tradition.

(c) The functions of Shakespeare's imagery require analysis. We can distinguish three main functions. (i) All imagery is used to assist in clarifying the meaning of the passage in which it occurs. Some imagery has no further use. This is most frequently true of such as is likely to have been employed unconsciously either because it is commonplace ("*fortune*, on his damned quarrel *smiling*" (*Macbeth*, I, ii, 14)) or because it is glanced at in passing and not dwelt on ("those honours *deep and broad* wherewith Your majesty *loads* our house" (*Macbeth*, I, vi, 17))— these two images do not form a 'mixed metaphor' in the bad sense, partly because they are so lightly touched on and also because they are treated intellectually, not sensuously). (ii) Sometimes imagery has the further function of establishing character (the most obvious instance is the exotic imagery in the speeches of Othello); (iii) sometimes it helps to elucidate a theme (the analogies from sub-human nature in *Lear* and *Macbeth*, which relate to the theme of order and disorder in the universe). I doubt whether the evocation of 'atmosphere' is an independent function; it is rather, I think, a by-product of thematic development—intellect and emotion were not separated in Elizabethan consciousness.

Perhaps we might consider more closely the relation of imagery to character and theme, since there are still occasional attempts to treat Shakespeare's dialogue naturalistically and the true significance of his imagery can never be appreciated on a basis of naturalism. Naturalism demands that no character shall use an image which would not be used by such a person in real life. Polixenes's reference to Judas Iscariot (*Winter's Tale*, I, ii, 419) and Macbeth's "poor player" (v, v, 24) would both be impossible to a naturalistic writer. If Shakespeare had been deliberately aiming at naturalism, he could scarcely have fallen into these errors by unconscious anachronism: he would be unlikely to associate Macbeth's Scotland with the drama, or, if this be not conceded, even Shakespeare would not naturally expect Gospel references from a pagan king. The case for naturalism collapses if it is punctured at any point, since a mixture of naturalism and conventionalism—which I have always believed to be Shakespeare's method —is itself conventional. The use of verse makes naturalism virtually impossible, even apart from the fact that people do not naturally talk in verse. The naturalistic playwright of to-day does not use his own prose style for all his characters indifferently; he attempts to write his dialogue in a variety of prose styles approximating to the styles which such persons would use in real life. He cannot often write in his own best prose, because usually his characters will be narrower in sensibility than he is himself. I believe that Shakespeare did sometimes write in a style inferior to his best in order to individualize his characters through the verse put into their mouths. He did so most notably with Othello and Iago. Othello's verse, noble as it is, has not the usual range and flexibility of Shakespeare, and Iago's pedestrian style is commonly recognized. But *Othello* was in this respect an experiment; thereafter Shakespeare rejected the method of characterization through verse style except in certain usually minor instances, such as the Shepherd in *The Winter's Tale*. It would be intolerable for a poet to have constantly to limit his poetic range to that of minds simpler and more stereotyped than his own: we can understand why Shakespeare for the most part preferred to use prose for less exalted characters and moods and, when writing verse, writes in his own style. Moreover, Shakespeare's method even in *Othello* is radically different from that of the naturalistic writer. Apart from its being in verse, the speech of Othello is not such as it would be in real life. He is a soldier, without the courtly refinements, rude in his speech,[1] as he says himself. Shakespeare suggests the much-travelled soldier in the exotic imagery of the Othello speeches, and the broad simplicity of syntax suggests a simple nature. But the eloquent poetry is of the medium, not the character. You cannot keep poetry out of poetic drama because the characters are not intended to be poetic themselves. Character may be suggested through the quality of the poetry, but in the nature of the case the one attribute that cannot be poetically expressed is that of poetic imagination. Those critics who still talk of the poetic imagination of Othello or Macbeth have surely not sufficiently meditated on the nature of Shakespeare's medium. We cannot judge the degree of a character's poetic imagination by the quality of his utterance; we must rely for such a judgement on direct indications. Othello is rude in his speech because he says so and it is what we would expect from what we know of his life and character; he has some imagination if he invents the handkerchief story, and a strong visual imagination helps to plague him in his jealousy; but there is nothing especially 'poetic' about him. To talk of Othello's poetic nature because he speaks of Anthropophagi, Arabian trees and turbaned Turks is to fall victim to a crude aesthetic. It is not the items mentioned, however romantic, that constitute poetry but the way in which they are treated. The famous Cydnus speech of Enobarbus depends considerably for its powerful effect upon the contrast between the luxurious barge and the everyday commercial associations of the "wharfs" and 'market-place" (*Antony and Cleopatra*, II, ii, 218, 220). Unless we are to ascribe to the character the composition of his own speech, we cannot claim him as 'poetic'. If we go so far as to allow Enobarbus an eye for luxurious appointments we have reached the limit of legitimate psychological induction.

Even the exotic imagery that Othello uses cannot, in the conventional framework of poetic drama, be claimed as revealing directly his mental operations. What it does is suggest his varied experience of foreign travel and the romantic aura which that cast about him. He is not a poet, nor necessarily highly imaginative, but he is seen to be a hero who would appeal to the romantic imagination of others. It is true, however, that many of the images employed are such as an Othello might well have used in real life. In contrast the magnificent imagery of *Antony and Cleopatra*—imagery of the heavens and the "ranged empire" (I, i, 34)—is not necessarily such as would naturally fall from the lips of a real-life Antony or Cleopatra. The poetry is not an outcome of their characters but their characters are created by the poetry. Indeed, the same imagery and the same poetic quality is given to other characters when speaking about them: to the unlikely Enobarbus, to a casual entrant such as Scarus, even to Octavius on occasions, though he has normally a well-marked 'deflated' style of his own. Thus we may conclude that Shakespeare's technique is not primarily naturalistic. He does certainly use imagery to help in characterization, but even then works more by poetic suggestion than by psychological realism. We can, however, distinguish in this connexion between images with a basis of naturalistic justification and those which have only poetic propriety. Shakespeare employs both types.

The remarks about *Antony and Cleopatra* lead to another consideration. Frequently imagery used in characterization refers not to the character of the speaker but to the person spoken about. When Octavius, in speaking about Antony or Cleopatra, uses the Antony-Cleopatra style we are not to ascribe their qualities to him. If we do we shall make nonsense of the play. An audience attuned to poetry will not be thinking of the speaker at such a time. When Valentine reports that Olivia will

> ...water once a day her chamber round
> With eye-offending brine: all this to season
> A brother's dead love, which she would keep fresh
> And lasting in her sad remembrance—   (*Twelfth Night*, I, i, 29)

we are to note how a ceremonial lustration with holy water—which is made with an admixture of salt—'fades into' the salting of beef for winter consumption. I do not think we are to admire the wit of Valentine or speculate on his religious leanings or association with the stockyard; but Olivia's mourning is seen for what it is, a sentimental and slightly ridiculous pose. Now the use of imagery to indicate the character of the person spoken about may itself involve a comment on the theme of the play, in this instance the theme of 'dream versus reality', the philosophic thread of *Twelfth Night*. So we may expect to encounter in the conventional drama of Shakespeare some groups of imagery which relate to theme rather than specifically to character, a use which I have already postulated and which I hope later to illustrate in detail. An immediate example is the theological reference of the Gentleman in *The Winter's Tale* to "a world ransomed, or one destroyed" (v, ii, 17); it has nothing to do with the speaker's character but everything to do with the underlying meaning of the play.[2] How are we to distinguish these uses of imagery? There are no rules; each instance must be treated separately in its context with all the resources of the critic's learning and sensibility. It is above all important that the first step should be in the right direction, that a proper distinction should be made between those images which have no significance outside their immediate grammatical and rhetorical function in the sentences in which they occur, and those which have a further significance either in relation to character or theme. To isolate a group of images and to deduce character or theme from them alone is to court every sort of freak interpretation. The images may be unconscious and their relationship to one another adventitious: the real significance of a chain of food images might be that Shakespeare had indigestion that morning. It is best to concentrate on those images which seem to express a quality of character or a theme for which there already exists good evidence of another kind (direct statement, implication of plot, etc.), or at least those which appear at important points in the development of the play and cannot be sufficiently accounted for in their immediate contexts. The truth is that no one method of approach to Shakespeare is adequate; the various approaches need to be balanced one against another.

2. APPLICATION

I propose to devote the rest of this essay chiefly to a consideration of the diabolic imagery in *Othello*, with some comparative study of *Macbeth* and *The Atheist's Tragedy*. Wilson Knight was, I think, the first to attempt what might be called a 'mystical interpretation' of *Othello*: his essay on "The Othello Music" in *The Wheel of Fire*[3] shows how the love of Othello and Desdemona is presented poetically in terms of heavenly bliss and cosmic order, while Iago figures as the devilish, disruptive force transmuting heaven into hell and order into chaos. Though I do not always agree with Knight's ingenious interpretations of Shakespeare's plays, I am surprised that this especially cogent essay has not received a greater measure of endorsement from other writers. The tendency is still to treat *Othello* purely as a domestic tragedy and to pay little attention to its profoundly theological structure.

With *Macbeth* it is different. Most recent critics agree in interpreting the later play, as I am bound to regard it, in the light of Christian theology. With whatever minor variations they take *Macbeth* to be a study of evil, the history of a soul's damnation. Consideration of the imagery, particularly as it relates to the doctrine of the Chain of Being, has done much to establish this interpretation. It has not yet been sufficiently realized, however, to what extent Shakespeare—deliberately, we must suppose—transformed the source-material of the play to give it theological precision. The renewed interest in Shakespeare's sources, which is a feature of contemporary scholarship, might well be directed to questions of this sort. Perhaps I may be allowed to give an example to which I have already drawn attention elsewhere. Holinshed, recounting the portents which accompanied the murder of Duff, states that "horsses in Louthian, being of singular beautie and swiftnesse, did eate their owne flesh, and would in no wise taste anie other meate". In *Macbeth* these become the King's own horses which, "turn'd wild in nature" and

> Contending 'gainst obedience, as they would make
> War with mankind,

"eat each other" (II, iv, 16). They are Duncan's horses so that there can be no doubt about where to apply the moralization of their behaviour. "Wild in nature" is a significant phrase: 'nature' is used many times in the play, frequently in connexion with ideas of order and disorder; wild nature to the Elizabethans meant disorder, nature escaped from the hand of man, her divinely appointed master. So the horses were "contending 'gainst obedience", against the graduated bond of duty and love which maintains the cosmic hierarchy; for them to "make War with mankind", a lower order in the Chain of Being against a higher, would imply rebellion, that most hideous word to an Elizabethan ear. As, however, the forces of evil, being centred in themselves and not in God, lack the cohesion which comes from mutual love and common duty, their power is limited and they ultimately turn to mutual destruction: Duncan's horses "eat each other". By comparing Shakespeare's words with those of his source we can thus see him defining and underlining the theological significance of the incident—and it becomes evident that the theology in Shakespeare's plays is not merely an unconscious reflexion of the age. The meeting of Malcolm and Macduff is usually said to be only a versification of Holinshed. Yet the scene (IV, iii) is full of religious imagery:

> new sorrows
> Strike heaven on the face;
>
> To offer up a weak poor innocent lamb
> To appease an angry god;
>
> Angels are bright still, though the brightest fell:
> Though all things foul would wear the brows of grace,
> Yet grace must still look so;
>
> Not in the legions
> Of horrid hell can come a devil more damn'd
> In evils to top Macbeth;
>
> I should
> Pour the sweet milk of concord into hell;
>
> Thy royal father
> Was a most sainted king: the queen that bore thee,
> Oftener upon her knees than on her feet,
> Died every day she lived;
>
> Devilish Macbeth
> By many of these trains hath sought to win me
> Into his power, and modest wisdom plucks me
> From over-credulous haste: but God above
> Deal between thee and me!

The description of Edward the Confessor and his touching for the Evil is full of religious imagery; St Edward is the positive contrast to "devilish Macbeth":

> He hath a heavenly gift of prophecy,
> And sundry blessings hang about his throne,
> That speak him full of grace.

When Ross arrives, Malcolm prays:

> Good God, betimes remove
> The means that makes us strangers!

So it continues:

> An older and a better soldier none
> That Christendom gives out;
>
> Not for their own demerits, but for mine,
> Fell slaughter on their souls. Heaven rest them now!
>
> Macbeth
> Is ripe for shaking, and the powers above
> Put on their instruments.

The scene is thus very full of religious images, several of them being direct references and so more likely to have been written deliberately. Not one of them, however, has any parallel in Holinshed. Shakespeare, it appears, had a habit of using religious imagery (including direct reference) which Holinshed—and how many others?—had not. It is not sufficiently accounted for by describing him as a typical Elizabethan.

It might be argued that *Macbeth* is a special case, being designed for a command performance before James I. There is a familiar list of the ingredients intended for his Majesty's pleasure: the good character of Banquo and references to his descendants, especially the show of kings; the 'equivocator' passage; touching for the King's Evil; the Scottish setting. The same intention might apply to the play as a whole. Not only is its demonology appropriate for the royal author of a treatise on that subject but the treatment of kingship (Duncan was "the Lord's anointed temple" (II, iii, 73)) and feudal hierarchy would appeal to the writer of the *Basilicon Doron*, while the strong theological flavour would surely win the approval of a king who notoriously enjoyed theological disputation and took the chair at the Hampton Court Conference with such manifest satisfaction. But these various ingredients are closely compounded; even the references to equivocation and the King's Evil take their place in the development of the theme. Shakespeare shows not only dramatic skill but a grasp of theology which could hardly be acquired for the occasion. Recent criticism of other plays, especially *Measure for Measure*, *King Lear* and the late romances, has revealed the same theological and philosophical concern, which I have myself also attempted to trace in the apparently alien atmosphere of *Antony and Cleopatra*.[4] If *Othello* should be found patient of a similar theological interpretation it would bring the play more into line with the other great tragedies.

Statistical methods are seldom satisfactory and never conclusive, but they can serve useful subordinate purposes.[5] I find thirty-seven diabolic images in *Macbeth*, i.e. images including such words as "hell", "hellish", "devil", "fiend", "fiend-like", "damn", "damned", or in some other way suggesting the notion of hell or damnation. In *Othello* I find sixty-four. *Macbeth* in the Globe Edition has 2108 lines and *Othello* 3316. A play the length of *Othello* with diabolic images occurring in the frequency of *Macbeth* would therefore have fifty-eight such images. Thus the frequency of their occurrence in *Othello* is greater even than in *Macbeth*, which recognizedly treats the theme of supernatural evil. There is something here, then, which calls for investigation. Every one has noticed the diabolic atmosphere of *Macbeth*, where "hell is murky" (V, i, 40) and its dun smoke (I, v, 52) hangs like a pall over the terrestrial scene. In *Othello* the image-hunter has been charmed by the exotic; the "antres vast and deserts idle" (I, iii, 140) have seized upon his imagination and distracted attention from the much more frequent and often no less vivid references to the "divinity of hell" (II, iii, 356). 'Exotic' is harder to define than 'diabolic', but, allowing for some subjectivity in interpretation, there are without doubt relatively few exotic images in *Othello*. I make the total fifteen[6] against the sixty-four images of hell and damnation.

The diabolic images in *Othello* cannot be adequately explained as purely local, exhausting their meaning in their immediate contexts. There are too many of them for that. Some are important direct statements, and several occur at turning-points in the drama, where they receive considerable emphasis. (This will appear later as we examine them.) Moreover, there is nothing in plot or characterization that is incongruous with their being given a wider significance. It appears, however, that they cannot primarily serve the purpose of characterization, either semi-naturalistically (like the exotic imagery of the Othello speeches) or by poetic convention. They can indeed be naturalistically justified, in that such expressions might be used on occasion by any one with a background of Christian thought—they are not out of character. But they are not characteristic of any particular person. They are widely distributed. Iago, surprisingly, has only eighteen to Othello's twenty-six; the remaining twenty are scattered among most of the other characters. Desdemona is the only important personage in the play to have none at all, and this, I think, has considerable significance for character: "O, the more angel she" (v, ii, 130). But they must have a more important function than the negative characterization of Desdemona.

Iago has only his fair proportion of diabolic imagery, yet we undoubtedly gain the impression that in this play the theme of hell, as it were, originates with him and is passed to Othello later as Iago succeeds in dominating his mind. Statistics show this impression to be well-founded. In Act I Iago has eight diabolic images and Othello none; in Act II he has six and Othello one. The change comes in Act III, where Iago drops to three and Othello rises to nine. In Act IV Iago has only one while Othello has ten, and in Act V Iago has none and Othello six. It all begins, then, with Iago.

Yet there is no obvious untheological reason why such imagery should be associated, either naturalistically or conventionally, with the type of character that Iago is meant to be. He has clearly much in common with the stage Machiavel; the fundamental principle he professes is that of pure self-interest:

> Others there are
> Who, trimm'd in forms and visages of duty,
> Keep yet their hearts attending on themselves,
> And, throwing but shows of service on their lords,
> Do well thrive by them and when they have lined their coats
> Do themselves homage: these fellows have some soul;
> And such a one do I profess myself. (I, i, 49)

To "do themselves homage", as the phrase itself brings out, is the very inversion of feudal duty, a deliberate throwing over of the old morality based on traditional religion. To ascribe "soul" to such fellows gives the word a new and shocking significance. Iago's practical materialism is evident in his attitude to love, "merely a lust of the blood and a permission of the will" (I, iii, 339), and in his contemptuous remark to Cassio, bewailing his wounded reputation: "As I am an honest man, I thought you had received some bodily wound" (II, iii, 266). But all this has been noted often enough. Except that Iago never openly expresses disbelief in God, the nearest parallel to his view of life is that of D'Amville in *The Atheist's Tragedy*:[7]

> Let all men lose, so I increase my gaine,
> I haue no feeling of anothers paine; (I, i, 144)

and

> All the purposes of Man
> Aime but at one of these two ends; pleasure
> Or profit. (IV, iii, 125)

36

D'Amville's whole life is based upon the belief that "there's nothing in a Man, aboue His nature" (I, i, 16), and, although Iago is less dogmatically blatant, his "'tis in ourselves that we are thus or thus" (I, iii, 322) implies an equivalent rejection both of divine providence and grace and of diabolic inspiration. D'Amville and Iago are alike in self-regard and philosophic egotism. Both are also consummate hypocrites. D'Amville poses as a man of religion; Iago, more subtly, as an "honest" man with a rough tongue and a tendency to cynical utterance that fail to conceal his essential goodness. Iago, as we have said, has nothing comparable to D'Amville's exclamation to Castabella: "Nay then inuoke Your great suppos'd protectour" (IV, iii, 173), nothing that directly denies the existence of God. But there is no occasion for it, and *The Atheist's Tragedy* is much more crudely polemic than *Othello*. Shakespeare, though he has more direct doctrinal statement than is usually credited to him, was too good a dramatist to employ such professions gratuitously: he prefers to show belief in action and express philosophy in its poetic equivalent. The beliefs already ascribed to Iago are made with sufficient point for him to be recognized by an Elizabethan audience as an 'atheist'. It may also be some indication of Shakespeare's intention for Iago that Edmund in *Lear*, his literary scion, professes to worship Nature as his goddess (I, ii, 1). Perhaps it may be objected that Iago believes at least in the Devil and that this implies his acceptance of the Christian scheme. Indeed, he dwells lovingly on the "divinity of hell":

When devils will the blackest sins put on,
They do suggest at first with heavenly shows,
As I do now.   (II, iii, 357)

But does Iago give the impression of believing in the powers of darkness in the way Macbeth does? He admires their "divinity"; he seems to enjoy being taken for a devil at the end when his machinations have been revealed; but there is never any hint that he has commerce with infernal powers. "'Tis in ourselves that we are thus or thus." "Thou know'st we work by wit, and not by witchcraft", he admonishes Roderigo (II, iii, 378). Iago is a self-made devil.

How, then, are we to understand the great number of diabolic images in *Othello*? They are related closely to Iago, but in what way? I do not think that there is any Elizabethan convention by which the Machiavel or atheist is presented in such terms. I find only fourteen diabolic images in the whole of *The Atheist's Tragedy*: some are merely oaths and the rest have no great significance for character nor are they used to develop a theme. In *Othello* those employed by Iago himself are capable of naturalistic explanation up to a point. We might find credible the character of an evil man who, though an unbeliever, likes to dwell on that aspect of religion which fills others with dread and to model himself upon a Devil in whom he does not objectively believe. Alternatively, we could accept Iago as a 'practical atheist', one who lives by an atheistic code without making any deliberate intellectual rejection of religion. There are many such. If this were so, his enjoyment of the devilish might colour his language without implying either belief or disbelief. If naturalistic consistency of character is desired, I suppose that either of these readings might supply it. But Shakespeare leaves us small leisure for such speculation when we are watching *Othello*. What he does, however, is to assail our ears with diabolic imagery throughout, and by no means only in the speeches of Iago. A naturalistic solution is not quite impossible. Accepting either of the naturalistic explanations given above for Iago's use of this sort of imagery, we might argue that the other characters as they come into the circle of his influence take over his forms of expression. But would any Elizabethan, even Shakespeare, entertain such a notion—or even conceive such a character as either of the 'naturalistic' Iagos I have projected? Since we have established that Shakespeare's method was fundamentally conventional, there is no need to accept a fantastic naturalistic explanation if a plausible conventional explanation lies to hand.

I shall argue that the diabolic imagery is used to develop poetically an important underlying theme. Of the sixty-four diabolic images in *Othello* not one occurs in Cinthio's *novella*. We have found Shakespeare adding considerably to the number of religious images in the sources of *Macbeth* and sharpening those that were already there, so as to develop poetically a theological theme. Is it not likely that when he introduced a similar type of imagery into *Othello* it was with a similar purpose? There is a steady increase in the use of diabolic imagery from act to act, which looks like thematic development. The figures for each act are, respectively, ten, eleven, thirteen, fourteen, sixteen. I shall outline what I believe to be the general function of this imagery in *Othello* and then consider its operation in detail.

Othello can be interpreted on three levels, the personal, the social and the metaphysical. In *Lear* and *Macbeth* these three levels are so closely interrelated that it is impossible to make sense of the personal or story level without taking the others into consideration. In *Othello* the interrelationship is less complete: the story can be considered alone, with the result that the other elements often remain unnoticed. Unfortunately without them the story itself is liable to misinterpretation. On the personal level we have a straightforward domestic tragedy—Cinthio's *novella*, in fact, with modifications. On the social level we have a study of a contemporary problem, the clash between the 'new man' thrown up by certain aspects of Renaissance culture, the atheist-Machiavel with his principle of pure self-interest, and the chivalric type, representing the traditional values of social order and morality. That Iago is more intelligent than Othello reflects the usual ambivalence of Shakespeare's judgement. On the metaphysical level we see Othello and Iago as exemplifying and participating in the age-long warfare of Good and Evil.

These various planes of meaning coalesce into something like unity. It appears that to Shakespeare Cinthio's ensign suggested (*a*) the contemporary atheist-Machiavel, and (*b*) the Devil himself. It seems to follow that Shakespeare thought of the 'new man', with his contempt for traditional morality and religion, as a disintegrating force seeking to break down the social order that is a part of cosmic order—as, in fact, an instrument (no doubt unconscious) of the Devil in his constant effort to reduce cosmos to chaos. This would be a very natural attitude for a conservative Elizabethan, and to express this attitude is one main function—a general function —of the diabolic imagery in *Othello*: Iago is a "demi-devil" (v, ii, 301), worse than an ordinary devil, a bastard one,[8] and his philosophy is a "divinity of hell".

But Shakespeare's metaphysical interest is not wholly absorbed in the social issue. The problem of good and evil is also presented for itself and in much the same terms as we are familiar with from modern interpretations of *Macbeth*. L. C. Knights has drawn attention to the theme of "the deceitful appearance" in the later play.[9] Good and evil are so readily confused by fallen humanity: "Fair is foul, and foul is fair" (*Macbeth*, i, i, 11). "There's no art", says Duncan, "To find the mind's construction in the face" (i, iv, 11). This same theme of deceitful appearance

38

runs its course right through the tragedies from *Hamlet* with its smiling villain to the final statement of *Macbeth*. In *Lear* Cornwall suspects Kent of being a sort of Iago:

> These kind of knaves I know, which in this plainness
> Harbour more craft and more corrupter ends
> Than twenty silly ducking observants
> That stretch their duties nicely. (II, ii, 107)

I do not think that the ramifications of deceitful appearance in *Othello* have ever received comment. Of course there is Iago—"honest Iago" (II, iii, 177), who is in truth a "hellish villain" (v, ii, 368) but only so revealed at the end of the play. Cinthio's ensign is described as *di bellissima presenza*, a fact which actors would do well to note, for Shakespeare surely intended Iago to have this beautiful exterior, since it fits so well with his other arrangements for 'deceit'. His hero, Othello, is a black man, as calculated, in those times, to inspire horror as Iago to inspire confidence. It was well known that the Devil frequently appeared in the form of a black man to his worshippers. "There's no art To find the mind's construction in the face." Contrary to a 'Neoplatonic' doctrine much entertained at the time,[10] Othello and Iago are in appearance the exact opposite of their natures. Ironically enough, they both agree at one point that "men should be what they seem" (III, iii, 126, 128). Why, again, is Michael Cassio a Florentine? There is nothing in Cinthio to that effect. The Florentines were noted for their fine manners, a quality displayed by Cassio: "'tis my breeding That gives me this bold show of courtesy" (II, i, 99). Florence was also known as the birthplace of Machiavelli and a special degree of subtlety seems to have been ascribed to his fellow-citizens.[11] Cassio is an exception. His exclamation upon Iago, "I never knew A Florentine more kind and honest" (III, i, 42), has several layers of irony and reveals his own simplicity, which is evident also in the drunken scene. Expectation is again disappointed. Even Desdemona deceives expectation: though a Venetian, she is not a "cunning whore" (IV, ii, 89) as Othello was led frantically to believe. The cunning whores of Venice were well enough known to Elizabethan England: "the name of a Cortezan of Venice is famoused over all Christendome", says Coryate in his *Crudities*.[12] An Elizabethan audience might have expected fickleness in her, not chastity. Yet, though she "deceived her father", a point which is stressed (I, iii, 194; III, iii, 206), and tells a white lie about the handkerchief, she is the most innocent of all deceivers, dying with a noble lie upon her lips: "Nobody; I myself" (v, ii, 124). Emilia with her materialistic code ought to be a fitting wife for Iago, but her cynical professions conceal a golden heart—which is what Iago pretended about himself. Deceitful appearance thus characterizes all the main figures in *Othello*. Where is the evil one? Who is true and who is false? The play is a solemn game of hunt the devil, with, of course, the audience largely in the know. And it is in this game that the diabolic imagery is bandied about from character to character until the denouement: we know the devil then, but he has summoned another lost soul to his side.

It begins with Iago. In his opening speech he refers to Cassio as "a fellow almost damn'd in a fair wife" (I, i, 21). We know nothing of the wife and I do not find much significance in the phrase, except as an example of Iago's perversion of values. Perhaps Shakespeare originally intended to introduce Cassio's wife into the plot but omitted her on deciding to use Bianca. "Damn'd" is not important here—I shall try to avoid the image-hunter's fallacy of treating all similar images as equally significant in spite of their context. A more interesting remark occurs shortly afterwards: "I am not what I am" (I, i, 65). Iago expresses his policy of Machiavellian deceit in a parodied negation of the Scriptural words in which God announces his nature: "I am that I am" (Exodus iii. 14). His own diabolic nature is implied. I do not think that a point such as this is too obscure for an Elizabethan, bred on the Bible and trained in verbal wit, to have apprehended at a first hearing, especially if the actor knew what he was saying. Now comes the calling-up of Brabantio; Othello must be plagued with flies (I, i, 71). Edith Sitwell may be right in seeing a reference to the Prince of Flies,[13] though I should not wish to press the matter. (The association of flies with devils was ancient and well known: cf. "The multiplying villanies of nature Do swarm upon him" (*Macbeth*, I, ii, 11). The "summer flies" of *Othello*, IV, ii, 66 have no apparent relation to the diabolic imagery. If any connexion exists, it is surely unintentional and unimportant.) Iago warns Brabantio that "the devil will make a grandsire" of him (I, i, 91). In the same passage Othello is "an old black ram" (I, i, 88). Iago thus begins the 'devil-black man' reference which perhaps runs in Brabantio's mind later. The audience, not having listened to Othello yet, might be a little dubious about him. Almost at the same time, however, Iago takes the name of devil to himself: "you are one of those that will not serve God, if the devil bid you" (I, i, 108)—it is jocular, and meaningful only in the light of later developments. Its immediate value is that of iteration; the audience is being repeatedly assailed with the idea of the diabolic. A similar value, and no more, attaches to Iago's confidence to Roderigo: he hates Othello as he does hell-pains (I, i, 155). Brabantio, perhaps inspired by Iago's language earlier, accuses Othello: "Damn'd as thou art, thou hast enchanted her" (I, ii, 63)—the black man and black magic naturally falling together. But Othello has an opportunity of showing his true nature, first in preventing bloodshed and afterwards in his speech before the senate. The first endeavour to make a devil of the black man fails to convince the Duke and his senators and leaves the audience persuaded of his high character. No "practices of cunning hell" (I, iii, 102) have been employed. Desdemona "saw Othello's visage in his mind" (I, iii, 253), the sensible converse of popular 'Neoplatonic' theory; her love was unconstrained. So the Duke pronounces Othello "far more fair than black" (I, iii, 291), putting aside the deceitful appearance. Iago has suffered an initial defeat, but we hear him in good spirits rallying Roderigo: "If thou wilt needs damn thyself, do it a more delicate way than drowning" (I, iii, 360), hammering again on the theme of damnation. He calls on his "wits and all the tribe of hell" (I, iii, 364), and the Venetian scenes close with an ominous couplet:

> I have't. It is engender'd. Hell and night
> Must bring this monstrous birth to the world's light. (I, iii, 409)

On the shore at Cyprus Iago has a chance to vent his cynicism in the guise of entertainment. Women are "devils being offended", he says (II, i, 112), but the description would apply more appropriately to himself. There is a moment of high poetry when Othello and Desdemona meet after their safe passage through the storm:

> O my soul's joy!
> If after every tempest come such calms,
> May the winds blow till they have waken'd death!

And let the labouring bark climb hills of seas
Olympus-high and duck again as low
As hell's from heaven! If it were now to die,
'Twere now to be most happy.   (II, i, 186)

The tragic tempest[14] does indeed drive Othello's bark from heaven to hell; if he had died then in Desdemona's arms he would have been most happy. We move from exalted verse to the flat prose of Iago. What delight shall Desdemona have "to look on the devil?" (II, i, 229). The 'devil-black man' equation is revived for Roderigo's benefit. Cassio, too, is explained to be "a devilish knave" (II, i, 250). The limit of Cassio's devilry is reached the same night when he becomes successively possessed by "the devil drunkenness" and "the devil wrath" (II, iii, 297). Iago must have smarted under Cassio's eschatology: "there be souls must be saved, and there be souls must not be saved" (II, iii, 106), and "the lieutenant is to be saved before the ancient" (II, iii, 114). But he maintains his usual composure, no doubt taking comfort in the thought of the lieutenant's imminent downfall. Cassio, deprived of his rank, exclaims against drunkenness: "Every inordinate cup is unblessed and the ingredient is a devil" (II, iii, 311). "Come, come, good wine is a good familiar creature, if it be well used", says Iago reasonably, having just used it himself for a purpose devilish enough. Iago, it has often been observed, dominates the three night scenes; he is a Prince of Darkness and enjoys them thoroughly. Perhaps Shakespeare took a moment's thought before giving him the one appropriate exclamation as the bell rings out: "Diablo, ho!" (II, iii, 161). The second act ends as he concocts "divinity of hell":

When devils will the blackest sins put on,
They do suggest at first with heavenly shows,
As I do now.   (II, iii, 357)

Cassio was not a serious candidate for diabolic honours. His penitent self-accusations, the fact that he feels himself to have been possessed because he has been drunk and disorderly, serve merely to demonstrate the daily beauty of his life (v, i, 19). He has behaved badly, Iago apparently well. But the audience know the truth. Shakespeare has staged a pretty contrast between the apparent sinner and the hypocrite. Iago has not so far shared the stage very much with Othello, but we now pass to the main action, in which the handsome villain and his hideous but noble dupe stand together in the eye of the audience; fair face and black soul, black face and fair soul in double contrast. Desdemona is to become a devil to Othello, that Othello might become a devil in fact.

Perdition catch my soul,
But I do love thee! and when I love thee not,
Chaos is come again.   (III, iii, 90)

This is weighty irony at the turning-point of the play. When he loves her not, chaos does come again, his life is disintegrated, and perdition catches his soul. The Devil's aim, we remember, is to reduce order to its primal chaos once more. There is a microcosm-macrocosm parallel behind the image. Iago now goes to work to arouse Othello's jealousy:

O, what damned minutes tells he o'er
Who dotes, yet doubts, suspects, yet strongly loves!   (III, iii, 169)

It would be wrong to make anything of the frequent association, in this play, of hell and damnation with sex. Heaven is equally expressed in terms of sexual love. The association is due merely to the particular dramatic medium. The war of good and evil is fought out in this intimate domestic field, just as in *Macbeth* the battleground is a kingdom and the most important relationships are political. Iago is duly warned: "If thou dost slander her...nothing canst thou to damnation add Greater than that" (iii, iii, 368). When he is half convinced of Desdemona's infidelity, Othello exclaims at the thought of it: "Death and damnation!" (iii, iii, 396). It is more than an oath. He loses his heaven with his faith in her.[15] Iago takes up the theme: "damn them then, If ever mortal eyes do see them bolster..." (iii, iii, 398). At the end of the scene, Othello, fully persuaded, thinks of Desdemona as a devil while he confers upon Iago the coveted promotion:

> Damn her, lewd minx! O, damn her!
> Come, go with me apart: I will withdraw,
> To furnish me with some swift means of death
> For the fair devil. Now art thou my lieutenant.   (iii, iii, 475)

"Fair is foul, and foul is fair." Bemused by passion, Othello falls into the deep deceit of taking good for evil and evil for good.

At this point we can see how the study of imagery illuminates character problems, even when the imagery is not used for differentiation between characters. Iago is so strongly associated with the diabolic that we are justified in interpreting his character in terms of demonology. All his stated motives may be genuine, but the deepest, as Bradley saw,[16] is the desire to plume up his will (i, iii, 399). He is mastered by the sins which caused the angels to fall, Pride and Envy. He has already acquired, when the play opens, an habitual evil which is expressed in opposition to whatever is good and beautiful. Destruction is the only form of self-assertion left to the proud and envious. The diabolic imagery and the aura it casts about Iago cause the insinuation of jealousy into Othello to take something of the form of a temptation and fall. At bottom Othello's sin is the sin of Adam (as in *Paradise Lost*): he allows passion to usurp the place of reason. On the night of the brawl he felt passion assaying to lead the way (ii, iii, 207). But Othello was expert in the command of soldiers; he never really lost self-control and so remained in control of the situation. In domestic affairs he was less expert; he had not formed habits of prudence and discretion in a way of life that was new to him. So passion had its way, in the form of jealousy, and like the Pontic sea (iii, iii, 453) rushed on blindly to its end. He is to seek swift means of death for Desdemona, whom he sees as a "fair devil". The fair devil, however, is at his side. "I am your own for ever", says Iago (iii, iii, 479), but it is Othello who has handed his soul into Iago's keeping. Confused by passion, Othello is on the devil's side without knowing it. Or perhaps he does know in part, for he has already called up "black vengeance from the hollow hell" (iii, iii, 447).[17]

With a totally false view of her nature, Othello finds "a young and sweating devil", in Desdemona's palm (iii, iv, 42). The importance of the handkerchief is underlined, for the audience as well as Desdemona:

> To lose't or give't away were such perdition
> As nothing else could match.   (iii, iv, 67)

42

"Perdition catch my soul": the handkerchief is central to the plot, and "perdition" to the argument. For a while the devil makes sporadic and rather casual appearances, important only because they keep the word dinning in the audience's ears. Iago compares a cannon to the devil (III, iv, 136); Cassio bids Bianca throw her vile guesses in the devil's teeth (III, iv, 184). The fourth act opens with a more serious passage:

> Naked in bed, Iago, and not mean harm!
> It is hypocrisy against the devil:
> They that mean virtuously, and yet do so,
> The devil their virtue tempts, and they tempt heaven. (IV, i, 5)

Ironic because, in spite of his morality, the devil has tempted Othello's virtue and he has fallen— into the sin of jealousy. When Othello drops down in a fit, his last words are "O devil!" (IV, i, 43). Iago continues to play upon him:

> O, 'tis the spite of hell, the fiend's arch-mock,
> To lip a wanton in a secure couch,
> And to suppose her chaste! (IV, i, 71)

(Bianca keeps up the theme for the audience: "Let the devil and his dam haunt you" (IV, i, 153).) At this stage Othello thinks continuously of Desdemona as a devil or a damned soul; this is the measure of his spiritual blindness, his enslavement by Iago: "Ay, let her rot, and perish, and be damned to-night" (IV, i, 191). His exclamations in the presence of Lodovico show how the thought has taken possession of his mind: "Fire and brimstone!" (IV, i, 245); then, as he strikes her, "Devil!" (IV, i, 251); and immediately after, "O devil, devil!" (IV, i, 255). This phase reaches its height in the terrible scene in which he treats Desdemona as a whore and her chamber as a brothel. Emilia, protesting her mistress's innocence, calls down "the serpent's curse" (IV, ii, 16) on the hypothetical beguiler of Othello, but alone with his wife he bids her swear her innocence and damn herself (IV, ii, 35),

> Lest, being like one of heaven, the devils themselves
> Should fear to seize thee: therefore be double damn'd:
> Swear thou art honest. (IV, ii, 36)

He is fully alive to the deceitful appearance; only he ascribes it to the wrong person: "Heaven truly knows that thou art false as hell" (IV, ii, 39). Even Patience, the "young and rose-lipp'd cherubin" must "look grim as hell" upon her fault (IV, ii, 63).[18] When he summons Emilia again it is as portress of hell (IV, ii, 90). The connexion with *Macbeth* is not irrelevant. The Devil is at work in Desdemona's chamber, not in the way Othello imagines but as surely as in the castle of Macbeth and with as bloody an outcome.

There is now a lull in the diabolic imagery except for another outburst of Emilia against the unknown villain who has poisoned Othello's mind. When Desdemona prays "If any such there be, heaven pardon him!" she retorts: "A halter pardon him! and hell gnaw his bones!" (IV, ii, 136). The irony of this, spoken in her husband's presence, is strong enough to link up with the denunciations of Iago later. Act IV, scene iii, the 'willow' scene, has no diabolic images, for Shakespeare is a master of decorum. It is more remarkable that Act V, scene i, Iago's last nocturnal scene of devilish activity, should produce only one reference of this kind, when the dying Roderigo recognizes the truth at last: "O damn'd Iago! O inhuman dog!" (v, i, 62). The murder of Desdemona is carried out, again appropriately enough, without any diabolical imagery: it is a moment for sympathy, not moral judgement. Thus between Othello's departure from Desdemona's chamber after the 'brothel' incident and Desdemona's last words to Emilia from her death-bed there are only two instances of diabolic imagery. In addition to the matter of local propriety this lull prepares very effectively for the continuous torrent of such imagery with which the play closes.

Hitherto the diabolic images have been frequently misapplied—to Othello in his innocence, to Cassio, to Desdemona. Now, immediately after Desdemona's death, the last misapplication is made and corrected. The same sort of images, with all the accumulated force of those that have gone before, will serve to give point and metaphysical depth to the denouement.

> *Oth.* She's, like a liar, gone to burning hell:
> 'Twas I that kill'd her.
> *Emil.* O, the more angel she,
> And you the blacker devil!
> *Oth.* She turn'd to folly, and she was a whore.
> *Emil.* Thou dost belie her, and thou art a devil. (v, ii, 129)

The formal stichomythia brings out the central importance of the passage. Desdemona quite certainly is angel, not devil, and she has gone to heaven. The imputation has passed from her to Othello, who this time can worthily sustain it. The black man is, after all, a devil: he has earned the title. He himself, however, still believes in the justice of his cause:

> O, I were damn'd beneath all depth in hell,
> But that I did proceed upon just grounds
> To this extremity. (v, ii, 137)

His illusion is soon to be done away. Emilia challenges Iago and, when he maintains Desdemona's guilt, roundly accuses him of telling "an odious, damned lie" (v, ii, 180). Othello, not yet believing her, attempts to justify himself to Gratiano, whose only reply is to invoke Desdemona's father, now dead:

> did he live now,
> This sight would make him do a desperate turn,
> Yea, curse his better angel from his side,
> And fall to reprobation. (v, ii, 206)

It is to have that effect upon Othello.

Meanwhile the master devil must be identified:

> Let heaven and men and devils, let them all,
> All, all, cry shame against me, yet I'll speak, (v, ii, 221)

says Emilia. When Iago's deceitful appearance has been penetrated at last, there is an end of the game. The devil stands revealed. This is sufficiently emphasized. "O cursed slave!" says Othello (v, ii, 276), and later:

> I look down towards his feet; but that's a fable.
> If that thou be'st a devil, I cannot kill thee. (v, ii, 286)

44

Iago, wounded, accepts the imputation with what seems like vindictive satisfaction: "I bleed, sir; but not kill'd" (v, ii, 288). Montano calls him "damned slave" (v, ii, 243), and Lodovico has a variety of epithets of the same type: "damned slave" (v, ii, 292); "damned villain" (v, ii, 316); "hellish villain" (v, ii, 368). But Othello's "demi-devil" (v, ii, 301) is the most appropriate. Prospero explains the term as he applies it to Caliban: "For he's a bastard one" (*Tempest*, v, i, 273).[19] Iago has not quite the stature of a devil, for the devils *believe* and tremble.

As for Othello, he too has become willy-nilly of the Devil's party:

> when we shall meet at compt,
> This look of thine will hurl my soul from heaven,
> And fiends will snatch at it. (v, ii, 273)

This sounds definite enough, like a statement for the audience. The description of the torments of hell which follows seems to express not only Othello's present state of mind but his future fate:

> Whip me, ye devils,
> From the possession of this heavenly sight!
> Blow me about in winds! roast me in sulphur!
> Wash me in steep-down gulfs of liquid fire! (v, ii, 277)

In this speech he takes an eternal farewell of his heavenly Desdemona. Emilia's words have come home to him:

> This deed of thine is no more worthy heaven
> Than thou wast worthy her. (v, ii, 160)

His suicide, since he is a Christian, seals his fate. Shakespeare does not leave us in much doubt about the eternal destiny of his tragic heroes. Hamlet is attended to heaven by flights of angels. (It would be quite opposed to Elizabethan dramatic conventions for Horatio to be mistaken at this point about the hero's spiritual state.) This strengthens my conviction that the proper reading of the last act of *Hamlet* would see the Prince as returning to Denmark determined upon justice, but no longer desirous of revenge. That Claudius should be killed is a necessity, he sees, not only of personal but of social justice:

> is't not to be damn'd
> To let this canker of our nature come
> In further evil? (v, ii, 68)

He is confident that Providence ("there's a special providence in the fall of a sparrow" (v, ii, 230) and "a divinity that shapes our ends" (v, ii, 10)) will provide him an occasion to become Claudius's executioner. There are no more self-reproaches and no more feverish plots; Hamlet is quietly determined yet apparently quiescent. And, sure enough, the occasion is provided for him almost at once. This interpretation, which has been deeply influenced by the excellent analysis of G. R. Elliott in his *Scourge and Minister*,[20] would permit us to give full weight to Horatio's commendation—which I cannot imagine being uttered on the Elizabethan stage over a genuine avenger. Lear, after being bound upon his fiery wheel in this life, attaining humility and patience, is also fit for heaven. Macbeth's last stand, however, is no atonement for his sins: it is not manly but "bear-like" (v, vii, 2), beast-like. According to *The Governour* this is not fortitude but desperation; it has no moral value, for those who "hedlonge will fall in to daungers, from whens there is no hope to escape" are "rather to be rekned with bestes sauage, than amonge men whiche do participate with reason".[21] So Macbeth, though we may pity him, presumably goes to hell. The same with Othello. We may feel "the pity of it" (IV, i, 206), but the Elizabethans had a harder view of eschatology than is common to-day. After all, to the Middle Ages and to the century after the Reformation it seemed likely that the majority of people would go to hell. And the Elizabethans knew their ascetic theology: Othello shows no sign of penitence, only of remorse, which is another thing. How different is the behaviour of Leontes when he awakens from his jealous dream. Leontes prepares for a lifetime of penitent devotion, whereas Othello, self-willed to the last, commits the final sin of taking his own life. Shakespeare is no narrow moralist, and Cassio finds the motive for Othello's suicide in his greatness of heart (v, ii, 361). But Shakespeare was no sentimentalist either: even the great of heart might commit irrevocable sin. There is no contradiction between the feeling of sympathy and a recognition of objective justice in the Elizabethan mind. In *Othello*, as in all Shakespeare's plays, the deceitful appearance is torn away at the end: good and evil are seen for what they are; and, though one soul be lost,[22] good will triumph and order be restored. "Cassio rules in Cyprus" (v, ii, 332) and

> To you, lord governor,
> Remains the censure of this hellish villain. (v, ii, 367)

I would not have it thought that, in proposing three levels of interpretation for Othello and in crediting Shakespeare with a considerable consciousness of what he was about, I intend to countenance any allegorizing of the incidents. The three levels coalesce into one; the deeper meanings, social and metaphysical, are directly applicable to the human story and necessary for a full understanding of its purport. The diabolic images we have considered do not carry us away from the characters into a world of metaphysical speculation in which they have no part. Rather they serve the true purpose of poetic drama, to show the underside, as it were, of ordinary life.[23] It is precisely in such sordid and—to the outsider—trivial domestic quarrels that the Devil is busiest. Shakespeare usually works as a romantic, raising his audience to the cosmic significance of his theme by setting it in remote ages and in the courts of kings. In *Othello* he goes differently to work, showing that the old war of Good and Evil has its centre everywhere, not least in the private household. *Othello* is Shakespeare's *Family Reunion*.

NOTES

1. See my *Shakespeare and the Popular Dramatic Tradition* (Staples Press, 1944; reprinted 1948), p. 65.

2. See my *The Winter's Tale: A Study* (Staples Press, 1947), p. 102.

3. I owe to Knight's essay the outline of the metaphysical interpretation of *Othello* and some particular points noted later.

4. See *Shakespeare and the Popular Dramatic Tradition*, pp. 116 et seq.

5. In counting images I have taken the complete sentence as my unit; i.e. if two or more images occur in a single sentence they count as one. This avoids dispute as to where one image ends and another begins. There is nothing sacrosanct about the punctuation of the Globe Edition, which has been followed—or perhaps of any other edition—but the principal aim has been to secure a firm basis for comparison.

6. I followed the method already described in note 5. It is only fair to notice that the "antres vast", the Anthropophagi and so forth are crowded into a single sentence and count as one image.

7. The edition of Tourneur used for quotation and reference is that of Allardyce Nicoll (1929).

8. See the Arden Edition of *Othello*, ed. H. C. Hart, p. 251, note.

9. *How Many Children Had Lady Macbeth?* (1933), p. 34. The essay is reprinted in *Explorations* (1946), where the reference appears on p. 18.

10. The belief, widely held in Elizabethan times, that moral character determines outward appearance is a popular misconception of Neoplatonic doctrine. It is expressed in Spenser's *Hymne in Honour of Beautie*, ll. 127 ff.:

> "So euery spirit, as it is most pure,
> And hath in it the more of heauenly light,
> So it the fairer bodie doth procure
> To habit in, and it more fairely dight
> With chearefull grace and amiable sight."

11. Sugden's *Topographical Dictionary to the Works of Shakespeare and his Fellow Dramatists* (1925) has a general statement about Florentine manners and two quotations concerning subtlety. The latter have the air of expressing an accepted opinion.

12. (Glasgow, 1905) I, 401. See also Deloney's *Gentle Craft*, ch. 2; in the *Works*, ed. Mann (Oxford, 1912), pp. 77 *et seq.*

13. *A Notebook on William Shakespeare* (1948), p. 118. I have not included this image in my total, but I have included "I am not what I am", which is not strictly an image at all. These are, I think, the only doubtful cases.

14. For the association of tempest with tragedy and an interpretation of its use in *Othello* somewhat different from that which I suggest, see Wilson Knight, *op. cit.* pp. 120 *et seq.*

15. Cf. Wilson Knight, *op. cit.* p. 127.

16. *Shakespearean Tragedy* (1905), p. 229.

17. I desert the Globe Edition here and give the reading of the Folio, which receives additional confirmation from the general run of diabolic imagery.

18. Our examination of diabolic imagery helps here to settle a textual crux. "Cherubin" must refer, as Johnson says, to a personified Patience and not, as Hart would have it, to Desdemona (*v.* Arden Edition, p. 202, n.). Othello consistently regards Desdemona at this time as a devil, whatever her appearance (in l. 37 she is merely "*like* one of heaven"). While rejecting Hart's reading of the Folio's "I heere", viz. "I here", there is no need to accept Theobald's emendation, "Ay, there". "Ay, here" gives perfectly good sense and is faithful to the Folio ("I" = "Ay", as frequently). The previous "there" ("Turn thy complexion there") might mean either that Patience is to alter her usually soft features at the theme of Desdemona's infidelity or, perhaps, in looking upon Desdemona. With either meaning the change from "there" in l. 63 to "here" in l. 65 would be dramatically effective if accompanied by a gesture focusing the audience's attention upon Desdemona.

19. See n. 8 above.

20. Duke University Press: Durham, North Carolina, 1951.

21. Bk. III, ch. 9; p. 229 in the Everyman Edition.

22. If we accept the Folio reading in l. 347, "Iudean" instead of "Indian", the case for Othello's damnation is strengthened. It seems the more likely reading, since it fits so well into the general pattern of the religious imagery and its apparent significance. Othello, like Judas Iscariot, has cast away the pearl of great price; he has rejected Desdemona and in so doing has rejected heaven. Like Judas, he fell through loss of faith.

23. T. S. Eliot writes in similar terms of poetic drama in his Introduction to my *Shakespeare and the Popular Dramatic Tradition*.

IAGO—VICE OR DEVIL?

BY

LEAH SCRAGG

For a considerable time critics have traced the characteristics displayed by Iago back to the Vice, the artful seducer of the Morality plays. Alois Brandl in 1898 included Iago among the descendants of the Vice, although apparently associating that figure with the Devil:

If we follow the role of Vice in the other English tragedies of this period and the following decades, we still find Haphazard in 'Appius and Virginia' as well as Ambidexter in 'Cambyses' as representatives of the old Morality-type, i.e. as seducer and hypocrite. In Marlowe's Mephistopheles the original diabolic character of this figure once more reaches full expression; in Marlowe's black Ithimor, Shakespeare's Aaron and Iago it is still strongly to be felt;[1]

and Cushman in 1900, while showing the utter disparity between the nature of Vice and Devil, explicitly endorses Brandl's derivation of Iago from the former and would add other Shakespearean villains to the list:

Why not also add to these Edmund in *Lear*, Richard III, Don John in *Much Ado About Nothing* and Antonio in *The Tempest*?[2]

The most recent and convincing exponent of this view is Bernard Spivack (*Shakespeare and the Allegory of Evil*, New York, 1958), who examined the typical characteristics of the Vice, proved that figures displaying similar characteristics were found in a number of Elizabethan plays and having shown Iago possessed the same attributes, concluded that he was, in fact, a descendant of the Vice playing his traditionally motiveless role beneath a mask of motivated hostility. In this way, the difficulties encountered in the play, particularly the ambiguous nature of Iago's motivation, are seen as the result of an attempt to 'translate' the popular, but amoral, seducer of the Morality stage into realistic Elizabethan-Jacobean drama.

However, if the characteristics which are thought to be typical of the Vice, and which are used by these critics as a kind of hallmark to detect his literary progeny, were found before, during and after the period of the popularity of the Morality play in the figure of the Devil, it would be equally arguable that it is to the Devil, not the Vice, that Iago is indebted. In this case he would revert once more from the unmotivated seducer to the motivated antagonist—from the amoral to the immoral. In the first part of this article I shall therefore attempt to show that Vice-like characteristics are not restricted to amoral beings, and in the second to suggest that the evidence within *Othello* points to an association between Iago and the powers of darkness which at least confirms his moral nature, if not proving his derivation from a traditional stage presentation of the Devil.

I

The attributes which typify 'The Vice', the figure which emerged after 1500 from the group of vices engaged in the psychomachia of the early Morality plays, and which are said to characterize his descendants, are as follows.[3] He was a gay, light-hearted intriguer, existing on intimate terms with his audience, whom he invited to witness a display of his ability to reduce a man from a state of grace to utter ruin. He invariably posed as the friend of his victim, often disguising himself for the purpose, and always appearing to devote himself to his friend's welfare. He treated his seduction as 'sport' combining mischief with merriment, triumphing over his fallen adversary and glorying in his skill in deceit. So far the analogy with Iago is obvious. He provided for his audience both humour and homiletic instruction. Above all, he was an amoral being whose behaviour was completely unmotivated—he simply demonstrated the nature of the abstraction he represented. In this respect, as Spivack points out, the Devil and the Vice are completely distinct:

The purposes of the Devil are those of a complex moral being. The whole purpose of the Vice is to illustrate his name and nature and to reflect upon the audience the single moral idea he personifies. The former acts to achieve his desires, the latter only to show what he is. Between the two no ethical continuity is possible because in the nature of a personification there is nothing that is subject to ethical definition.[4]

But although entirely disparate ethically, in their dramatic presentation the Vice and the Devil have much in common, those characteristics which I have outlined as typical of the Vice being found in the Devil of the Mystery plays over a hundred years before the emergence of the allegorical figure—as the motivated antagonist who leaped on to the stage at York, pushing the audience aside, reveals:

> Make rome be-lyve, and late me gang,
> Who makis here all þis þrang?
> High you hense! high myght ȝou hang
> > right with a roppe.
> I drede me þat I dwelle to lang
> > to do a jape. (XXII, 1–6)[5]

This is the introduction to Satan's temptation of Christ in the wilderness, but the tones in which the Devil speaks are exactly those of the Vice, with his direct, familiar relationship with the audience, his vivacity and emphasis on what is to take place as a 'jape'. He too confides in the audience, relating the way in which he delights to bring men to eternal pain (XXII, 7–12), why he intends to tempt Christ—i.e. his motivation (XXII, 19–22), what he intends towards his victim (XXII, 39–42) and how he is going to attempt it (XXII, 43–8). In other words he invites us to witness a display of his boasted ability to bring men to sin. When he actually approaches Christ, he poses as his friend:

> Þou hast fasted longe, I wene,
> I wolde now som mete wer sene
> For olde acqueyntaunce vs by-twene,
> > Thy-selue wote howe.
> Ther sall noman witte what I mene
> > but I and þou. (XXII, 61–6)

The Devil is naturally unsuccessful and his actions are limited by the necessity of following the Biblical narrative, but nevertheless, in this earliest surviving dramatic presentation of a tempter on the English stage, the attitudes of the later Vice figure are already evinced. The intimacy with

49

the audience, the self-explanatory, demonstrative role for homiletic effect, the attitude to the attack on the spiritual welfare of the victim as 'sport', the device of posing as the friend of the person to be betrayed, are all present. The only, and very significant, difference lies in the fact that the Devil is implicitly and explicitly motivated. Since the York cycle was first presented between 1362 and 1376 and was played until 1568[6] this kind of antagonist was seen on the English stage long before the emergence of the Vice after 1500 and continued to be seen throughout the period of the popularity of the Morality play.

The Chester cycle, which probably originated between 1377 and 1382 and which was played until 1575, does not present such a vivacious Devil as the York plays but elements which are to be typical of the Vice may be seen—notably the emphasis on disguise:

> A manner of an Adder is in this place,
> that wynges like a byrd she hase,
> feete as an Adder, a maydens face;
> her kinde I will take; (II, 193–6)[7]

and the pose as the friend of the victim:

> Take of this fruite and assaie:
> It is good meate, I dare laye,
> and, but thou fynde yt to thy paye,
> say that I am false. (II, 233–6)

Similarly the attitude to the temptation of Christ as a game is still present:

> a gammon I will assay. (XII, 4)

The play of the Last Judgement in the Wakefield cycle (originated 1390–1410) also presents vivacious Devils eager to destroy their human victims. Their chief, Tutivillus, introduces himself on his first entrance, priding himself on his dexterity in entrapping the unwary (XXX, 211–21),[8] and commenting with cynical glee on the lasciviousness and general corruption of the times which give him his opportunity to win souls (XXX, 273–304). Although a Devil, Tutivillus does not comment in any way on the motive for his antagonism. He shows no cause for his hostility towards mankind—his whole being is involved in an attitude of merriment, almost glee, not hatred and resentment. His joyful, triumphant, imaginary welcoming of the sinners to hell is typical:

> ye lurdans and lyars / mychers and thefes,
> fflytars and flyars / that all men reprefes,
> Spolars, extorcyonars / Welcom, my lefes!
> ffals Iurars and vsurars / to symony that clevys,
>   To tell;
> hasardars and dysars,
> ffals dedys forgars,
> Slanderars, bakbytars,
>   All vnto hell. (XXX, 359–67)

He has the energy, life and homiletic function which are claimed to be typical of the Vice, together with his professional pride in his work:

I am oone of youre ordir / and oone of youre sons;
I stande at my tristur / when othere men shones.   (xxx, 207–8)

And like the Vice these Devils blend comedy and homiletics as they triumph over their fallen
victims:

Secundus Demon: Where is the gold and the good / that ye gederd togedir?
The mery menee that yode / hid*er* and thed*ir*?
   Tutiuillus: Gay gyrdyls, iaggid hode / prankyd gownes, whedir?
Haue ye wit or ye wode / ye broght not hider
Bot sorowe,
And youre synnes in youre nekkys.
   Primus Demon: I beshrew thaym that rekkys!
he comes to late that bekkys
youre bodyes to borow.   (xxx, 550–8)

The Devil is beginning to appear on the stage with the motive for his antagonism taken for
granted, while he simply exhibits his delight in evil and his dexterity in entrapping souls.

The Devil of the single pageant extant from the Newcastle plays, which originated before
1462 and were played until 1567–8, has similar characteristics. He exists on intimate terms with
his audience, confiding to them his plans to corrupt Noah's wife (lines 109–13).[9] He too exhibits
a light-hearted approach to his deception and insinuates himself into the confidence of his dupe.
His bland greeting to Mrs Noah, whom he hopes to destroy, 'Rest well, rest well, my own
dere dame' (line 115), might well have been spoken by innumerable later Vice figures.

Quires N,P,Q,R, of the *Ludus Coventriae*[10] (originated *c.* 1400–*c.* 1450) probably had a separate
existence before their inclusion in the cycle and the Devil of these sections is of a very different
kind from the demon filled with overt hatred found in other parts. He shares the characteristics
noted in earlier Devils, particularly the intimacy with the audience to whom he introduces
himself (26, 1–2), recounts with pride his aim in the world:

I am Norsshere of synne · to þe confusyon of man
To bryng hym to my dongeon · þer in fyre to dwelle   (26, 5–6)

and recites his past triumphs and his skill in entrapping souls (26, 23–4). He also confides to
them his plans for the destruction of Christ (26, 50–3), invites them to become his friends
(26, 61–3) and finally departs with a declaration of alliance (with obvious homiletic significance)
between himself and his listeners:

I am with ȝow at all tymes · whan ȝe to councel me call
But for A short tyme · my-self I devoyde.   (26, 123–4)

The Devil here has much in common with the Vice and clearly shows that Vice-like characteristics are not solely the province of amoral beings. The Devil, as Satan, also has a speech addressed
directly to the audience at the opening of Play 31, in which, having introduced himself, he
confides to the audience his fears about Christ, and outlines his plans for revenging the rebuff
given to him by Christ when he tempted him in the wilderness:

Þat rebuke þat he gaf me · xal not be vn-qwyt
Som what I haue be-gonne · & more xal be do

51

> Ffor All his barfot goying · fro me xal he not skyp
> but my derk dongeon I xal bryngyn hy*m* to.   (31, 486–9)

The Devil, the original motivated revenger of English drama addresses his audience here in tones very like those of innumerable self-explanatory villains of the Elizabethan stage. When the other Devils are appalled at the prospect of Christ coming to hell and Satan realizes that he has over-stepped himself, it is in terms of his 'sport' that he laments:

> A · A · than haue I go to ferre
> but som wyle help I haue a shrewde torne
> My game is wers *þa*n I wend here
> I may seyn · my game is lorne.   (31, 507–10)

Once more the Devil anticipates the Vice.

All that remains of the Norwich Mystery cycle are two versions of the pageant of Adam and Eve where the Devil appears simply as the Serpent. However in the version composed after 1565 he shows his kinship with the traditional tempter—taking his audience into his confidence and revealing to them his intention to disguise himself to further the temptation (lines 38–41).[11] The motive for the antagonism displayed by the Serpent is not commented upon; like Iago he simply 'can yt nott abyde, in theis joyes they shulde be'. Antagonism from the Devil, in whatever form he appears, is understood.

Thus in three out of the four major Mystery cycles extant (if the Chester cycle is regarded as a partial exception), as well as in those pageants surviving from the Newcastle and Norwich plays, the Devil shows many of the characteristics which typify the Vice, and which have been identified by Brandl, Cushman and Spivack as vestigial traces of the Vice in the self-explanatory villains of the Elizabethan–Jacobean stage with their curious combination of malice and merriment. It seems fairly safe to assume that these Devils were typical of those in the Mystery plays as a whole, which originated before the emergence of the allegorical drama, were performed throughout the period when the Morality play enjoyed its popularity, and, judging from the number of copies made at the close of the sixteenth century, would still have been familiar after they had actually disappeared from the stage.

However, the Devil was presented as the seducer of mankind in the Morality plays themselves before 'The Vice' as distinct from a number of vices, emerged into dramatic prominence. In the first complete Morality play extant, *The Castle of Perseverance* (1405–25), it is the Evil Angel, not the subsidiary vices, nor even The World or The Flesh, who is Humanum Genus's chief enemy. His method of seduction is the traditional one. He poses as man's friend supporting him against the 'bad' counsels of the Good Angel (IV, 340–8)[12] while instructing the vices on the means to be used to procure Humanum Genus's downfall (V, 547–51). But he is not simply the artful contriver of the hero's ruin—he also displays the irreverent humour and contempt for virtue shown by Spivack to be typical of the Vice, for example:

> ȝa ! wha*n*ne þe fox prechyth, kepe wel ȝore gees !
>   he spekyth as it were a holy pope.
> goo, felaw, & pyke of þe lys
>   þat crepe þer up-on þi cope !   (VI, 804–7)

52

—a speech addressed to the Good Angel! When Humanum Genus finally dies in sin, he triumphs over him as the Vice is to triumph over his victim and as Iago is to triumph over the fallen Othello.

Similarly, in *Mankind*[13] (1465–70), the second complete Morality play extant, it is not the vices—Nought, New-Guise and Now-a-days—who are Mankind's most potent adversaries, for he is easily able to repel them by beating them away; it is their cunning chief, Titivillus, who brings about his downfall. Mr Spivack devotes a long section to Titivillus (*op. cit.* pp. 123–5) showing, step by step, how his actions and speeches provide a pattern for the behaviour of a Vice,[14] but in fact, as Spivack barely notices, he is not a Vice at all. The playwright makes his nature perfectly clear when he declares, 'propy[r]lly Titiuilly syngnyfyes the fend of helle' (III, 879). He is not an unmotivated amoral figure representing an inner moral frailty, he is the motivated antagonist of Mankind, the moral being devoted to his spiritual destruction. It is true that the role he plays is soon to be taken over by the Vice because, as Mr. Spivack rightly observes, the Devil 'is not a personification but an historical figure out of Christian mythology and folklore, and an illogical intrusion, therefore, into the drama of abstraction' (*op. cit.* p. 132), but the dramatic qualities the Vice comes to represent are surely derived from him.

The Devil also acts as seducer in the third of the so-called Macro-morals, *Mind, Will and Understanding* (1450–1500). Here he enters immediately after Mind, Will and Understanding have been presented and in typical manner quickly takes the audience into his confidence, revealing who he is:

> I am he þat syn be-gane   (line 332)[15]

and what has motivated his animosity:

> My place to restore,
> God hath mad a man.   (lines 327–8)

In Vice-like manner he boasts of his cunning (lines 341–2) and then proceeds to share with the audience his intention to corrupt Mind, Will and Understanding, thus bringing the soul to damnation (lines 365–70). Most significantly, however, he disguises himself before proceeding to the temptation, showing once more that the disguise motif, associated with the pose as the friend of the victim, originated with the Devil:

> For, to tempte man in my lyknes,
> yt wolde brynge hym to grett feerfullness,
> I wyll change me in-to bryghtnes,
>   & so hym to be-gy[le].   (lines 373–6)

In the role of well-wisher, he then dupes the trio into believing that a life of prayer and contrition is not pleasing to God, brings them from piety to depravity and triumphs to his intimates, the audience, on his good success, while he proceeds, Iago-like, to tell the ultimate goal of his operation:

> That soule, God made in-comparable,
> To hys lyknes most amyable:
> I xall make yt most reprouable,
>   Ewyn lyke to a fende of hell.
> At hys deth I xall a-pere informable,
> Schewynge hym all hys synnys abhomynable,
> Prewynge hys soule damnable,
>   So with dyspeyer I xall hym qwell.   (lines 536–43)

Similarly in *Mary Magdalene* (c. 1480–1520), a curious combination of Mystery and Morality, it is the Devil, as Satan, who is once more the cause of the central character's downfall. He enters in the seventh scene to confide to the audience both the motive for his hatred of mankind and his desire for their destruction (lines 366–71).[16] It is he who initiates the attack on Mary Magdalene, inviting the help of The World and The Flesh, and his is the principal triumph and joy at the news of her downfall ('a! how I tremyl & trott for ʒese tydyng*es*!'). It is he who severely punishes his agents when Mary escapes his clutches and he who, with the Seven Deadly Sins under his command, provides the combination of temptation and comedy associated with the Vice.

John Bale's anti-catholic Mystery play *The Temptation of Our Lord and Saviour Jesus Christ by Satan* (1538) also gives a picture of a Satan who is a fitting heir to the traditional archetypal adversary of the Mystery stage. He enters immediately after Christ's first speech and proceeds to explain his name and function to the audience in the manner typical of the Vice. The only difference lies in the motivated hostility displayed:

> I am Satan, the common adversary,
> An enemy to man, him seeking to destroy
> And to bring to nought, by my assaults most crafty.
> I watch everywhere, wanting no policy
> To trap him in a snare, and make him the child of Hell. (p. 155)[17]

He then confides his fears of Christ's coming (p. 155) and reveals his purpose towards him. He intends to deceive him by guile and will adopt a disguise frequently used by Vices for the same purpose:

> I will not leave him till I know what he is,
> And what he intendeth in this same border here:
> Subtlety must help; else all will be amiss;
> A godly pretence, outwardly, must I bear,
> Seeming religious, devout and sad in my gear.
> If he be come now for the redemption of man,
> As I fear he is, I will stop him if I can. (pp. 155–6)

He then disguises himself as a hermit, approaches Christ and poses as one well-disposed towards him (p. 156). Having insinuated himself into his company, he begins to flatter him, to seem solicitous for his welfare, while at the same time trying to instil doubts into his mind beneath the cloak of friendship—just as Iago is later to plant seeds of doubt in the mind of his victim:

> Now, forsooth and God! it is joy of your life
> That ye take such pains; and are in virtue so rife
> Where so small joys are to recreate the heart: (p. 156)

—compare his exclamation on hearing how long Christ has fasted:

> So much I judged by your pale countenance. (p. 156)

In his attempt to persuade Christ to change the stones to bread, he emphasizes that his sole thought is upon the well-being of his friend:

> My mind is, in this, ye should your body regard;
> And not, indiscreetly, to cast yourself away. (p. 157)

54

1A *The Battle of Lepanto* (7 October 1571).
Engraving by Adrian Collært, after Johann Stradanus

1B *Desdemona cursed by her father.* Drawing by Delacroix

II *Desdemona cursed by her father.*
Oil painting by Delacroix

III Olivier as Othello, National Theatre, 1964

IVA *Othello*, St James's Theatre, London, 1951. Production by Orson Welles; decor by Motley.
'Soft you, a word or two before you go'

IVB *Othello*, Theatre of Olomouc, Czechoslovakia, 1951

A Edmund Kean

B Salvini

C Forbes-Robertson

D Frederick Valk

E Paul Robeson

F Orson Welles

G Godfrey Tearle

H John Gielgud

I James McCracken

V The visual presentation of Othello

VI Act II, scene i of the production of *Othello* at the Princess Theatre, 1861, with A. Fechter as Othello. Drawing reproduced from *The Illustrated London News*

VII Ellen Terry as Desdemona and Henry Irving as Othello in the *Othello* production at The Lyceum Theatre, 1881.
Illustration from *The Bill of the Play* for 1881.

Such at General Post Office as a Newspaper
VOL. XIII.—No. 329

SATURDAY, MARCH 18, 1876

PRICE SIXPENCE
Or by Post Sixpence Halfpenny

VIII Isabel Bateman and Henry Irving in *Othello*, at The Lyceum Theatre, 1876.
From an illustrated paper of 1876

IX John Henderson as Iago in Act III, scene iii of the *Othello* production at the Theatre Royal, Covent Garden, 1785

X *Othello*, Royal Shakespeare Theatre, 1971. Directed by John Barton, designed by Julia Trevelyan Oman, with music by Guy Woolfenden. Emrys Jones, as Iago, takes a photograph of (front row, l. to r.) David Calder as Cassio, Lisa Harrison as Desdemona, Brewster Mason as Othello, Bernard Lloyd and Miles Anderson as Soldiers and (back row, l. to r.) Anthony Langdon as Montano, Elizabeth Spriggs as Emilia, and Matthew Robertson as a Soldier

XIA *Othello*, Shakespeare Memorial Theatre, 1954. Produced by Antony Quayle; designed by Tanya Moiseiwitsch. Under the awning

XIB *Othello*, Shakespeare Memorial Theatre, 1956. Produced by Glen Byam Shaw, designed by Motley. Iago and the Moor

XII Edwin Booth as Iago, 1881

XIII Ralph Richardson as Iago and Edith Evans as Emilia in the Old Vic
production of *Othello*, 1932

(Crown copyright. Theatre Museum, Debenham Collection)

XIV Macready as Iago in the production of *Othello* at The Haymarket Theatre, 1838.
Illustration reproduced from an original painting by Tracey

XV Edmund Kean as Othello

XVI The Moorish Ambassador to Queen Elizabeth, 1600

His attitude throughout the temptation is that of an honest man showing his friend the 'folly' of his behaviour. He is the man of the world, offering his knowledge of things to the unrealistic idealist—the analogy with Iago is obvious:

> I put case: ye be God's son—what can that further?
> Preach ye once the truth the bishops will ye murther. (p. 157)

Compare:

> Alas! it grieveth me that ye are such a believer: (p. 164)

and

> If I bid ye make of stones bread for your body,
> Ye say man liveth not in temporal feeding only.
> As I bid ye leap down from the pinnacle above,
> Ye will not tempt God, otherwise than you behove.
> Thus are ye still poor; thus are ye still weak and needy: (p. 164)

and the supreme counsel of the down-to-earth man of the world, the counsel Iago gives Othello: renounce your faith, it is foolish:

> Forsake the belief that ye have in God's word,
> That ye are His son, for it is not worth a turd!
> Is he a father that see his son thus famish?
> If ye believe it, I say ye are too foolish.
> Ye see these pleasures—if you be ruled by me,
> I shall make ye a man: to my words, therefore, agree. (p. 164)

Defeated, Satan, the eternal antagonist, like Iago, vows eternal defiance:

> I defy thee...and take thy words but as wind. (p. 166)

This Devil with his pose of friendship, his man of the world attitude and his subtlety, is a direct pointer to the kind of Devil Iago is.

The Devil continued to appear, sporadically, as the antagonist of mankind throughout the history of the Morality play. He was the chief enemy of Youth in *Lusty Juventus* (1547–53), he had a less important role as Satan in *All For Money* (1559–77) when the transition from allegorical to literal drama had begun, and, while the Morality play was foundering in the closing decades of the century, he took new life as Mephistophilis in *Dr Faustus* (1588–92).

Thus not only did the Devil possess many of the characteristics of the Vice long before the emergence of the latter figure (such Devils as Titivillus anticipating the Vice in every respect), he continued to appear on the stage as tempter throughout the history of the Morality play. Moreover, a number of plays show that in fact a certain confusion between the respective roles of Vice and Devil existed in the minds of at least some Tudor dramatists. In *The World and The Child* (1500–22), when Conscience hears that Manhood has been seduced by the Vice, Folly, he exclaims:

> Lo, sirs, a great ensample you may see,
> The frailness of mankind,
> How oft he falleth in folly
> Through temptation of the fiend: (p. 267)[18]

which suggests that even if Folly does not partake of the nature of the Devil, he somehow acts under his guidance. Similarly, in Bale's *Three Laws of Nature, Moses and Christ* (1538), Natural Law exclaims to the Vice, Infidelity,

> I defy thee, wicked fiend. (p. 15)[19]

This Vice is called 'fiend' more than once in the course of the action and Natural Law declares that he shuns his company as he would 'the devil of hell' (p. 16). Confusion of this kind is most apparent in the 1578 edition of *All For Money*. In addition to the usual stage directions this edition provides elaborate instructions for the costumes of the various characters, including:

> Here commeth in Gluttonie and Pride dressed in deuils apparel. (B iii r)[20]

Later in the same play we are told that 'Here all the deuilles departe' (B iiii r) when it is clear that Satan, Gluttony and Pride have gone out. Ethically disparate as they undoubtedly are, the Vice and the Devil have a similar function and share a fund of common characteristics which makes confusion between their dramatic roles possible.

Finally, the Devil was still seen on the Elizabethan and Jacobean stage long after the decline of both Mystery and Morality play—*Grim the Collier* (1600), *The Merry Devil of Edmonton* (1599–1604), *If it Be Not Good, The Devil is in it* (1611–12), *The Birth of Merlin* (1597–1621), etc., all testifying to the perennial popularity of the figure of the supreme antagonist. For, ultimately, it is the Devil who, in Christian myth, and thus in Christian drama, is the implacable enemy of mankind. The Vice, the allegorical representation of an inner moral frailty, takes over the role of seducer in the Morality play, but he continues to show the traditional attitude to the part—the intimacy with the audience, the self-revelation, glee, irreverence, triumph over the fallen victim, etc. Freed from the confines of the Biblical narrative and the limitations of a narrowly defined moral status, he is able to develop these characteristics to a more marked degree, and by virtue of his amoral demonstrative nature and consequent detachment from the fate of his victims, he is able to pass naturally and easily, as Spivack has shown, into non-allegorical farce. But, fundamentally, the operation of the Vice is the operation of the Devil adapted to fulfil the needs of the dramatized psychomachia, and it is as the Devil that the figure passed into Elizabethan and Jacobean drama. If, therefore, the characteristics Iago displays were derived from an earlier figure, it seems extremely likely that it is to the Devil rather than the Vice that he is indebted, and that far from being a basically motiveless, amoral figure, he is a motivated being, engaged in the pursuit of some kind of revenge.

II

There is much evidence in *Othello* to confirm the suggestion that Iago is related, in some way, to the powers of darkness, and critics have long commented upon the diabolism that surrounds the figure of the 'villain' and invests the imagery of the play. Coleridge called Iago 'a being next to devil, and only not quite devil',[21] Bradley disputed the point[22] and modern critics continue to argue the question. Among those who support the view (in one way or another) that Iago partakes of the nature of the Devil, Stoll has pointed to the ambiguity of his motivation:

None of the motives at which Iago glances—the grievance in the matter of the promotion, or his lust for Desdemona, or his fancy that Othello or Cassio may have played him foul with Emilia—is sufficient for the vast villainy of his nature...

and concluded that:

He is a son of Belial, he is a limb of Satan.[23]

Wilson Knight has seen the play as a cosmic battle for the soul of man with Iago as a 'kind of Mephistopheles',[24] Maud Bodkin sees Iago as an archetype of the Devil, defining 'Devil' as 'our tendency to represent in personal form the forces within and without us that threaten our supreme values',[25] and S. L. Bethell analysing the distribution of the diabolic imagery in the play concludes that:

The play is a solemn game of hunt the devil, with, of course, the audience largely in the know. And it is in this game that the diabolic imagery is bandied about from character to character until the denouement: we know the devil then, but he has summoned another lost soul to his side.[26]

Heilman, discussing Iago's loss of humanity and the function of the serpent imagery in this respect, has suggested the way in which Iago's diabolism functions in the play:

As Iago's diabolism thus emerges distinct from the interwoven texture of action and language, we see how the myth of the devil enters into the play—not as a formula which squeezes out the individuality of Iago, nor as a pure idea of which the dramatic parts are an allegorical projection, but as an added dimension, a collateral presence that makes us sense the inclusiveness of the fable.[27]

But against this view stands Dr Leavis with his famous pronouncement that Iago is no more than 'a necessary piece of dramatic mechanism' designed to trigger off Othello's jealousy,[28] and Marvin Rosenberg who emphasizes Iago's humanity (showing him to be a recognizable psychological type) and repudiates his fiendishness[29] in spite of the fact that his study of the stage history of the play shows that Iago's role is most powerful when played, as Macready played it, as 'a revelation of subtle, poetic, vigorous, manly, many-sided devilry'.[30]

To attempt to analyse the diabolic element in the play when this has been done so fully by the critics cited would be superfluous, but for the purpose of this article it is necessary to summarize very briefly the evidence in support of the view that the myth of the Devil does enter, at some level, into the play. From the very opening of the action, Iago's relationship with the powers of darkness is continually emphasized—it is towards hell that he looks constantly for inspiration, hell and the Devil are for ever in his mouth, continually invoked by him; compare

> Hell and night
> Must bring this monstrous birth to the world's light   (I, iii, 397–8)

with:

> Divinity of hell!
> When devils will the blackest sins put on,
> They do suggest at first with heavenly shows,
> As I do now: (II, iii, 339–42)

and

> I do hate him as I do hell pains   (I, i, 155)

where his very tones suggest familiarity with the pains he speaks of. Examples could be multiplied. As Heilman has shown, when Othello falls a victim to Iago's temptation, he catches from him not only his debased view of life but his field of reference:

57

> Damn her, lewd minx! O, damn her, damn her!
> Come, go with me apart; I will withdraw
> To furnish me with some swift means of death
> For the fair devil. (III, iii, 479–82)

> Naked abed, Iago, and not mean harm!
> It is hypocrisy against the devil. (IV, i, 5–6)

> Fire and brimstone! (IV, i, 228)

The word 'devil' is passed constantly from mouth to mouth. Much of the action of the play seems to take place in the darkness and horror of hell itself—the confusion and darkness of the night scene before Brabantio's house, the quarrel during the night watch, the attempted murder of Cassio—scenes of darkness and mischief over which Iago presides like an evil genius. But it is the final scene of the play that provides the most convincing evidence for Iago's diabolism when the accumulated reference of the play is finally crystallized and centred on him as Othello, in a moment of terrible clarity, realizes the truth:

> I look down towards his feet—but that's a fable.
> If that thou be'st a devil, I cannot kill thee. (v, ii, 289–90)

His failure to do so and Iago's derisive reply,

> I bleed, sir; but not kill'd (v, ii, 291)

surely provide a comment on Iago's ultimate nature. Othello, at least, has no doubts about the nature of the deception that has been practised on him.

> Will you, I pray, demand that demi-devil
> Why he hath thus ensnar'd my soul and body? (v, ii, 304–5)

Indisputably Iago is engaged in the elaborate seduction of a representative of mankind and the destruction of the values that he represents. But although he undertakes this attack with joy, almost light-heartedness, he reveals that, however gleeful he is in pursuing the downfall of his victim, his hatred of him, of the virtues he possesses, is malevolent in the extreme. Note the intensity of the hatred in the following:

> I follow him to serve my turn upon him. (I, i, 42)

> So will I turn her virtue into pitch;
> And out of her own goodness make the net
> That shall enmesh them all. (II, iii, 349–51)

> If Cassio do remain,
> He hath a daily beauty in his life
> That makes me ugly. (v, i, 18–20)

These are not the tones of an amoral figure acting under the necessity imposed by dramatic convention to demonstrate his own nature, but the accents of a moral being impelled by a burning desire to feed fat a consuming hatred with revenge.[31]

But if Iago is to be regarded on one level (Heilman's 'added dimension') as a Devil rather than a Vice, his famous motives may no longer be regarded as the realistic trappings designed to cloak his allegorical origins, and fit him for the literal stage. They must be organic rather than functional. The proposition that Iago is a Devil in some sense of the word[32] implies that it is his nature to envy those whose character or situation is in any way superior to his own, to suffer from a sense of injured merit and to seek to destroy anything which by its very superiority threatens his self-love. Hence, locally, he feels he has been slighted by Othello in the promotion of Cassio, he asserts that Othello and Cassio have cuckolded him from his conviction that they cannot be as virtuous as they appear, and from his diseased belief that he is being constantly slighted. His 'love' for Desdemona is his desire to possess that object which is clearly highly desirable and belongs to someone else. But the ultimate motive for his hatred of Othello, Desdemona, and Cassio is his denial of the values they affirm, his fixed opposition to the virtues they represent. It is the hatred of Satan for the sanctity of Adam and Eve, the hatred of a being who is forced to recognize a virtue he cannot share and constantly desires. Hence the 'daily beauty' of the lives of Othello, Cassio, and Desdemona is a constant affront to him. The myth of Satan depicts him as falling from heaven from a sense of being undervalued; he tempted Adam and Eve both because they were superior to him, and therefore an object of envious hatred, and because he desired to avenge a supposed injury. Iago's motivation is very similar. At the close of the play, when he has corrupted Othello's mind, destroyed both him and Desdemona, when, for them, Paradise has been lost, Iago is dragged away to the tortures that are his element. He does not die at the end of the play, he is not to be put rapidly to death. He is to linger in pain like the powers of whom he is the instrument. Iago follows the pattern laid down in the garden of Eden and repeated over and over again in Christian literature by the archetypal adversary of mankind. Antagonistic to all forms of virtue, obscurely envying a state he constantly denies, he is the inveterate opponent of virtue, the seducer of mankind, who reduces his victims by guile from their original state of bliss to grief, death and hell.

It is clear that the characteristics displayed by Iago could well have been derived from the Devil rather than the Vice and that this proposition is reinforced by the emphasis on devilry in the play and the nature of Iago's attitude to his victims. But it would be overstating the position to assert categorically that Iago's characterization is *necessarily* derived from a traditional stage presentation of the Devil. All that can be claimed is that the Devil's claim to be Iago's forefather is at least as good as that of the Vice, and is supported by evidence in the play. Thus, while the Devil cannot be proved to be Iago's ancestor, his contradictory claim clearly invalidates the view that Iago *must* be regarded as a descendant of the Vice because of the dramatic characteristics he displays. Literary origins make dubious discussion at best, and it would be highly lamentable for Iago to be deprived of his motivation on the grounds that he is an amoral survivor from the psychomachia, roughly clad in the garments of realism, when the very characteristics which have reduced him to this exigency, together with the corroborative evidence from the play, suggest that he is not a Vice but a Devil.

© LEAH SCRAGG 1968

59

NOTES

1. *Quellen des weltlichen Dramas in England vor Shakespeare* (Strassburg, 1898), p. xciv.

2. 'The Devil and The Vice in the English Dramatic Literature before Shakespeare', *Studien zur englischen Philologie*, Heft VI (Halle A. S., 1900).

3. This summary is drawn from Mr Spivack's analysis of the figure.

4. Spivack, *op. cit.* p. 134.

5. References are to *York Plays*, ed. Lucy Toulmin Smith (Oxford, 1885).

6. The dates of all plays are those given in *Annals of English Drama 975–1700*, by Alfred Harbage, revised by S. Schoenbaum (1964).

7. References are to *The Chester Plays*, Part I, ed. Hermann Deimling, E.E.T.S. *E.S.* LXII (1892).

8. References are to *The Towneley Plays*, ed. George England and Alfred W. Pollard, E.E.T.S. *E.S.* LXXI (1897).

9. References are to the text of this play included in *The Non-Cycle Mystery Plays*, ed. Osborn Waterhouse, E.E.T.S. *E.S.* CIV (1909).

10. References are to *Ludus Coventriae* or *The Play called Corpus Christi*, ed. K. S. Block, E.E.T.S. *E.S.* CXX (1922).

11. References are to the text included in *The Non-Cycle Mystery Plays* (see n. 9 above).

12. References are to the text in *The Macro Plays*, ed. F. J. Furnivall and Alfred W. Pollard, E.E.T.S. *E.S.* XCI (1904).

13. A text of this play may be found in *The Macro Plays* (see n. 12 above).

14. Cp. 'The pivotal action of the allegorical drama, repeated as many times almost as there are plays, is a more sophisticated version of just such a demonstration and such a lecture' (Spivack, *op. cit.* p. 125).

15. References are to the text of the play included in *The Macro Plays* (see n. 12 above).

16. References are to the text of the play in *The Digby Mysteries*, ed. F. J. Furnivall, The New Shakespeare Society (1882).

17. References are to *The Dramatic Writings of John Bale*, ed. John S. Farmer, Early English Drama Society (1907).

18. References are to *Dodsley's Old English Plays*, vol. I, ed. W. Carew Hazlitt (4th ed. 1874).

19. See n. 17 above.

20. Cp. *All For Money*, Old English Drama, Students Facsimile Edition (1910).

21. *Notes and Lectures upon Shakespeare*, ed. Mrs H. N. Coleridge (1849), I, p. 262.

22. Lecture VI (Othello), *Shakespearean Tragedy* (St Martin's Library, 1957), pp. 185–6.

23. *Art and Artifice in Shakespeare* (Cambridge, 1933), p. 97.

24. Cp. 'The Othello Music' in *The Wheel of Fire* (1930).

25. Cp. *Archetypal Patterns in Poetry* (Oxford Paperbacks, 1963), p. 223.

26. Cp. 'Shakespeare's Imagery: The Diabolic Images in *Othello*', p. 39 above.

27. Cp. *Magic in the Web* (Lexington, 1956), p. 96.

28. Cp. 'Diabolic Intellect and the Noble Hero' in *The Common Pursuit* (Peregrine Books, 1962), p. 138.

29. Cp. *The Masks of Othello* (Berkeley and Los Angeles, 1961), pp. 170–1.

30. *Ibid.* p. 124.

31. Rosenberg's study of the stage history of *Othello* is again illuminating here, for he shows that Iago's role is unsatisfying when played as Vice rather than Devil. Thus an Iago of 1912 'tended to be impish rather than devilish…the real venom…seldom emerged' (p. 156) and Maurice Evans failed in the part because 'young, open of countenance, light and gay of speech and step' as his Iago was, his evil lost its point, was 'too much akin to *irresponsible mischief making*' (my italics). He was clearly amoral rather than immoral.

32. He has been variously regarded as a Devil on the metaphysical level, as a Devil incarnate, as a man possessed, and as a man in the process of becoming a Devil by the denial of the basic facts of his humanity.

OTHELLO, LEPANTO AND THE CYPRUS WARS

BY

EMRYS JONES

In 1604 the theatrical company for which Shakespeare wrote and acted was taken under the patronage of the new king; and it is becoming increasingly clear that at least two of the plays written by Shakespeare during the early years of the new reign were probably intended to reflect James I's opinions and tastes.[1] *Othello*, acted at court on 1 November 1604, seems never to have been considered in relation to Shakespeare's new patron. I want to suggest that, like *Measure for Measure*, *Macbeth*, and possibly other plays written during these years, *Othello* was also designed as a work appropriate to the chief dramatist of the King's Men.

James's various interests as a man, theological, political and scholarly, as well as his multiple roles as king—in particular his peculiar historical position as the first *British* king of modern times—provided panegyrists with a number of possible themes. He could be celebrated for his wisdom and learning, his piety, and his love of peace, as well as for the British unity which his accession to the English throne had achieved. Allusions could be made to his views on the theory of kingship and on witchcraft, and his own published works, *Basilikon Doron* and *Daemonologie*, could be searched for usable material. In poems, masques and processions he could be figured as David, Solomon, Augustus or Brute. There was also one other aspect of James's public personality which was eagerly taken up at the time of his accession: he could be acclaimed by poets as one of themselves. For while still a young man in Scotland James had not only written but published poems, so that along with his other roles he could be celebrated as a poet-king—and poets in particular were naturally anxious that no one should forget the fact. A sonnet by Drayton addressed to James opens, 'Of Kings a Poet, and the Poets King', and an epigram of Jonson's calls him 'best of Poets'. Of course other English monarchs of recent date had also written poetry: Henry VIII and Elizabeth I had done so. But their poems had been no more than brief lyrics, while James's poetical works were more ambitious. Among the poems and translations which he had published the best known was his original heroic poem *Lepanto*. It is this poem, I suggest, which provides the link between *Othello* and the king.

Lepanto was first published in James's second volume of verse, *His Maiesties Poeticall Exercises at Vacant Houres*; the earliest known edition is dated 1591. It was written several years before, probably in 1585, when James was nineteen.[2] The poem is hardly of much interest in its own right; yet whatever its poetic deficiencies it had at least the merit of a striking subject: an heroic action taken from recent history and of large political importance.[3] James's poem celebrates the great naval victory over the Turks won by the confederate Catholic states. The battle of Lepanto was the culmination of a military episode which had begun in 1570 with the Turkish attack on Cyprus, at that time one of Venice's richest territorial possessions. Spain and Rome, who were in a confederation with Venice, came to her assistance, and in the autumn of 1571 the combined Christian fleet of Spain, Venice and the Papacy set sail from Messina under the command of

Don John of Austria, the illegitimate half-brother of Philip II. Battle was joined with the Turkish fleet at the gulf of Lepanto (near Corinth) on Sunday 7 October 1571. There were heavy losses on both sides, but the greater part of the entire Turkish fleet was destroyed or captured. Lepanto was not only an overwhelming victory for the Christians: it was also the only great Christian victory over the Turks in the sixteenth century. It was usually interpreted as a victory for Christendom as a whole, Protestant as well as Catholic, and so, although the king of a fiercely Protestant nation, James could take it as a suitable theme for his Christian muse.

James's *Lepanto* quickly became famous. Poets and scholars in England paid it tribute; Du Bartas translated it into French. In his edition of James's poems James Craigie collects a number (27 in all; the collection is not exhaustive) of contemporary references to James as a poet; among the writers are Sidney, Gabriel Harvey, Francis Meres, Sir William Alexander, and Ben Jonson.[4] Some of them refer explicitly to *Lepanto*: e.g. Gabriel Harvey, who in *Pierces Supererogation* (1593) declares of James that he

hath not only translated the two diuine Poems of Salustius du Bartas, his heauenly Vrany, and his hellish Furies, but hath readd a most valorous Martial Lecture vnto himselfe in his own victorious Lepanto, a short, but heroicall, worke, in meeter, but royal meeter, fitt for a Dauids harpe—Lepanto, first the glory of Christendome against the Turke, and now the garland of a soueraine crowne.

As might have been expected, there was a sharp revival of interest in James's poem—as there was in all his published works—at the time of his accession to the English throne. A separate edition of *Lepanto* was printed in London in 1603; the poem was called on the title-page *His Maiesties Lepanto, or, Heroicall Song*. *Naupactiados*, a Latin version of *Lepanto* by Thomas Moray, appeared in 1604. In *Sorrows Joy* (1603), a collection of elegies for Elizabeth I and panegyrics to James, a poem by 'T.B.' asks what poet is worthy to praise the King and answers, predictably enough:

Lo then the man which the *Lepanto* writ;
Or he, or els on earth is no man fitt.[5]

And in the same year, 1603, Richard Knolles dedicated his *Generall Historie of the Turkes* to James, and in his dedicatory epistle argued the aptness of the dedication: 'and the rather, for that your Maiestie hath not disdained in your *Lepanto*, or *Heroicall Song*, with your learned Muse to adorne and set forth the greatest and most glorious victorie that ever was by anie the Christian confederate princes obtained against these the *Othoman* Kings or Emperors.'

There is further evidence that James was especially famed as a poet for *Lepanto*, and also that the poem was made to contribute to the coronation celebrations of 1604—possibly the year in which *Othello* was composed. In March 1604 the King made a coronation progress through the City of London. (The ceremony was described by Dekker in his tract, *The Magnificent Entertainment given to King James*.) The *Italians Pageant*, one of several before which the King and his party were required to pause, consisted of a great triumphal arch inset with illustrative panels.[6] The main panel on the front side of the arch depicted James's main claim to the English throne by showing James receiving the sceptre from Henry VII. On the reverse side of the arch James's *poetic* achievements were the subject:

The middle great Square, that was aduanc'd over the *Freeze* of the Gate, held *Apollo*, with all his Ensignes and properties belonging vnto him, as a *Sphere*, *Bookes*, a *Caducaeus*, an *Octoedron*, with other

Geometricall Bodies, and a Harpe in his left hand: his right hand with a golden Wand in it, poynting to the battel of *Lepanto* fought by the Turks, (of which his Maiestie hath written a Poem) and to doe him Honour, *Apollo* himselfe doth here seeme to take vpon himself to describe...

Othello was probably the first of Shakespeare's tragedies to be written for the King's Men, but it has apparently never been related to this setting of allusive compliment. That this is so may be largely due to the peculiarly private or even domestic nature of its action. Among Shakespeare's mature tragedies *Othello* is exceptional in taking its main plot not from history but fiction; and its apparent confinement to the private and domestic sphere sets it apart from *Hamlet*, *King Lear*, *Macbeth* and the Roman tragedies. Indeed its difference from them has seemed so marked that it has often been described as Shakespeare's closest approach to domestic tragedy, a *genre* concerned not with the crimes and misfortunes of heads of state but with the essentially private, and so unhistorical, lives of citizens. However, the opening scenes of the play present a world which could not be at all adequately described in private and domestic terms. These scenes evoke a world of public events: affairs of state, war, and military heroism. This is the world in which history is made; and it is accordingly in this part of the play—the Venetian part—that *Othello* comes closest to the public and historical concerns of the other tragedies.

The early Venetian scenes are usually regarded as a prelude to the main Cyprus action. The conflict of Othello and Brabantio can be seen as foreshadowing the much more difficult, because concealed and oblique, conflict of Othello and Iago, just as the trial scene in I, iii can be seen as anticipating the passing of judgement that takes place in the last scene of all. But otherwise the political events of which we hear in Act I are usually regarded as no more than dramatic machinery for effecting the move of the main characters from Venice to Cyprus (which from one point of view they are) and are seldom scrutinized for their own sakes. The modern playgoer probably never spares a thought for the 'Cyprus wars' mentioned early on by Iago or for the manoeuvres of the Turkish naval forces which so much exercise the Duke and Senators of Venice. The question arises whether Shakespeare had any further intentions in including this political material.

Shakespeare has so arranged it that the night of Othello's elopement with Desdemona is also the night when the news arrives in Venice of the movements of the warlike Turkish fleet. The Venetian Senate is alarmed for the safety of Cyprus, and accordingly Othello is sent to Cyprus to supervise its defences. Now although these events are in themselves fictitious (since Othello is a fictitious character), they could hardly have failed to arouse the memory of anyone in Shakespeare's audience who was at all aware of recent European history. For if we were to seek to give an approximate date to the action of *Othello*, we should be driven to the crucial years round about 1570, the year of the Turkish attack on Cyprus. The Turks had landed in Cyprus in 1570; one of the two chief Cypriot towns, Nicosia, soon fell; the other, Famagusta, underwent a long siege. It was these events which led to the Lepanto engagement. But the victory of Lepanto did not in fact restore Cyprus to Venice. Famagusta fell to the Turks on 1 August 1571, which left them in possession of the island. At the time of *Othello*'s composition therefore (*c.* 1602–4), Cyprus had been in Turkish hands for over thirty years.

The connexion of the action of *Othello* with these events, at least in approximate date, is allowed by the *Variorum* editor. He quotes Isaac Reed's note on the play:

63

Selymus the Second formed his design against Cyprus in 1569, and took it in 1571. This was the only attempt the Turks ever made upon that island after it came into the hands of the Venetians (which was in the year 1473), wherefore the time of the play must fall in with some part of that interval.[7]

In the story by Cinthio, which is Shakespeare's only known source of *Othello*, there is no mention of a Turkish threat to Cyprus. Cinthio's story was after all written before the Turkish attack; the *novelle* were first published in 1565. So the story of Cinthio's Moor takes place in time of peace. If Cinthio was in fact his only narrative source, then Shakespeare has deliberately brought the action closer to the events of 1570–1. In Act I everything seems—or perhaps would have seemed to Shakespeare's first audience—to be moving towards the naval action which culminated in Lepanto and which was fought over the same issue as that presented in the play: the possession of Cyprus. Thus Iago says of Othello in the opening scene:

> . . .he's embark'd,
> With such loud reason to the Cyprus wars,
> Which even now stand in act. . .

—a remark which seems, among other things, to be a direct pointer ('Which even now stand in act') to the approximate date of the action. And in the senate scene the Duke tells Othello:

> The Turk with a most mighty preparation makes for Cyprus.

Given the fame of the battle of Lepanto, Shakespeare's audience could not have been blamed if they had expected the play to run along lines much more true to history than the play they were actually given. But what happens is that as soon as the main characters are arrived in Cyprus, the action moves into an entirely fictive realm, and the military background involving Venice and Cyprus, Christian and Turk, is allowed to recede from the attention. The military and naval clash which we seem led to expect never takes place. For instead of a battle between Christians and Turks Shakespeare substitutes a storm which disperses the Turkish fleet. An anonymous Gentleman announces:

> News, lads! Our wars are done.
> The desperate tempest hath so bang'd the Turk
> That their designment halts. . .

A little later, on his entry, Othello dismisses all thought of the Turks in a single line:

> News, friends: our wars are done; the Turks are drown'd.

And finally the war theme is allowed to die with the Herald's proclamation:

It is Othello's pleasure, our noble and valiant general, that, upon certain tidings now arriv'd, importing the mere perdition of the Turkish fleet, every man put himself into triumph. . .

The fate of the Turks is left purposely vague, and apart from one or two phrases which help sustain the atmosphere of an exposed garrison town ('this warlike isle', 'what! in a town of war, / Yet wild, the people's hearts brimful of fear'), the Turkish threat to Cyprus is allowed to be forgotten.

The connexion of *Othello* with the 'Cyprus wars' is not only of a general kind; there are one or two precise details which suggest that Shakespeare had the events of 1570–1 in mind. At the beginning of I, iii the Duke and Senators are comparing the different reports of the numbers of the Turkish galleys and their movements:

> 1 *Senator*. My letters say a hundred and seven galleys.
>
> *Duke*. And mine a hundred and forty.
>
> 2 *Senator*. And mine two hundred...

In his *Generall Historie of the Turkes* Knolles says of the Turks at the time of their first landing in Cyprus: 'The whole fleet at that time consisted of two hundred gallies.' And later, after Lepanto, he notes: 'Of the enemies gallies were taken an hundred threescore and one, fortie sunk or burnt.'[8] The Turks had two hundred galleys; and this is the number which Shakespeare keeps last, in a position of emphasis or climax, for his Second Senator. This may be a coincidence, but at any rate the size of the Turkish fleet in *Othello* and at Lepanto was roughly the same. A little later in the same scene a messenger reports news of the Turkish movements:

> The Ottomites, reverend and gracious,
> Steering with due course toward the isle of Rhodes,
> Have there injointed them with an after fleet.
> > 1 *Senator*: Ay, so I thought. How many, as you guess?
> > *Messenger*: Of thirty sail; and now do they restem
> Their backward course, bearing with frank appearance
> Their purposes toward Cyprus.

These movements correspond exactly to Knolles's account of the Turkish invasion plans:[9] 'For *Mustapha*, author of that expedition...had before appointed *Piall Bassa* at a time prefixed, to meet him at the RHODES, and that he that came first should tarrie for the other, that so they might together sayle into CYPRUS.' Knolles goes on to say that Mustapha Bassa 'together with *Haly Bassa* and the rest of the fleet, departed from CONSTANTINOPLE the six and twentieth of May, and at the RHODES met with Piall as he had before appointed. The whole fleet at that time consisted of two hundred gallies...'[10]

Shakespeare could of course have taken for granted a general interest in the Ottoman empire which is very remote from what a modern audience brings to *Othello*. The Turkish menace to Christendom was a fact of Shakespeare's entire lifetime; it remained of pressing concern to the West until late in the seventeenth century. This fact may of itself have given *Othello*'s Cypriot setting an ominous character which is lost on us. As Knolles put it: 'The Venetians had ever had great care of the island of CYPRUS, as lying far from them, in the middest of the sworne enemies of the Christian religion, and had therefore oftentimes determined to have fortified the same.'[11] So Cyprus could be seen as an outpost of Christendom, rich, vulnerable, and perilously situated: a highly suitable setting for a play showing Christian behaviour under stress. After Cassio's drunken brawl has been put down, Othello is to say:

> Are we turn'd Turks, and to ourselves do that
> Which Heaven hath forbid the Ottomites?
> For Christian shame, put by this barbarous brawl.

His words, skilfully placed in the scene, are emphatic and ironic. For if Shakespeare's fictitious action can be said to belong to the years 1570–1, those were historically the very years when

Cyprus underwent a violent conversion from Christian to Turkish rule—the years when it literally 'turned Turk'.

However, over thirty years had elapsed between Lepanto and the writing of *Othello*. The battle in itself was no longer a matter of topical interest as it had been (for example) to Gascoigne when, in his Mountacute Masque of 1572, he had incorporated a dramatic eyewitness account of the sea-fight. But in the interval between 1571 and 1604 an event had taken place which had had the effect of reviving interest in the battle, at least indirectly. The event was, as I have argued, the accession of James, whose heroic poem was promptly reprinted in 1603.

It has to be admitted that Shakespeare seems to have no direct indebtedness to James. What is relevant here is Lepanto as an historical event rather than any specific reminiscences of the poem.[12] Even so the general affinities between *Othello* and *Lepanto* are sufficiently striking. Both are concerned, *Lepanto* centrally, *Othello* peripherally, with the 'Cyprus wars', which for Shakespeare's contemporaries could only have pointed to the events of 1570–1. And a major topic of the poem—the conflict of Christian and Turk—is present in *Othello* as it is in no other of Shakespeare's plays. Knolles's dedication of his *Generall Historie of the Turkes* has already been quoted; it can surely be assumed that Shakespeare and his fellow actors would have been quite as adroit in publicly saluting their new patron.

© EMRYS JONES 1968

NOTES

1. See Henry N. Paul, *The Royal Play of 'Macbeth'* (New York, 1950); David L. Stevenson, 'The Role of James I in Shakespeare's *Measure for Measure*', *E.L.H.* XXVI (1959), 188–208; Josephine Waters Bennett, '*Measure for Measure*' *as Royal Entertainment* (New York and London, 1966); I have argued the case for *Cymbeline* in *E.C.* XI (1961), 84–99.

2. *The Poems of James VI of Scotland* (vol. 1), ed. James Craigie (Edinburgh and London, 1955), p. xlviii.

3. The subject inspired several Venetian painters. Paolo Veronese's *Battle of Lepanto* is reproduced in Samuel C. Chew's *The Crescent and the Rose. Islam and England during the Renaissance* (New York, 1937). Chew quotes (p. 126) Jonson's *Cynthia's Revels*, IV, i, 48 ('He looks like a Venetian trumpeter in the battle of Lepanto in the gallery yonder') as evidence for the existence of paintings on the subject in England.

4. Craigie, *op. cit.* Appendix A.

5. Quoted by Craigie, *op. cit.* p. 276.

6. *The Dramatic Works of Thomas Dekker*, ed. Fredson Bowers (Cambridge, 1955), II, 262–5.

7. *Othello*, ed. H. H. Furness (Philadelphia, 1886), 357. The editor wrongly attributes the comment to Henry Reed, author of *Lectures on English History and Tragic Poetry* (1856). It should be attributed to Isaac Reed; it occurs in his prefatory note to *Othello* in his edition of Shakespeare (1799–1802).

8. Knolles (2nd edn. 1610), pp. 846, 863.

9. This was noted by Isaac Reed.

10. Knolles, *op. cit.* p. 846.

11. Knolles, *op. cit.* p. 847.

12. In '*Othello*' *as the Tragedy of Italy* (1924), an attempt at a cryptic reading of the play, Lilian Winstanley wrongly states (p. 21) that the battle of Lepanto is directly referred to. In this context of the Christian and Turkish conflict in *Othello*, see F. N. Lees's article, '*Othello's Name*' (*N.Q.*, n.s., VIII (1961), 139–41), for the suggestion that Shakespeare adapted Othello's name from that of Othoman, the founder of the Ottoman (or Othoman) empire. Shakespeare could have found an account of Othoman in Knolles.

OTHELLO AND THE PATTERN OF SHAKESPEARIAN TRAGEDY

BY

G. R. HIBBARD

The twelve lines that conclude *Othello* provide an ending that is radically different from the ending of any other of the tragedies. Lodovico's main concern is with Iago and his punishment. There is no formal praise of the hero, the only tribute he receives being Cassio's laconic comment on his suicide: 'For he was great of heart.' His body, and that of Desdemona, are not carried off in state, but hurriedly hidden from view by the drawing of the curtain around the bed on which they lie, because the spectacle they offer is felt as something monstrous and obscene. Nothing is left to be settled and disposed of except the house and fortunes of the Moor, which pass in one brief clipped sentence to Gratiano, Desdemona's next of kin. No interpretation of the events that have led up to the disaster is given, or even promised. Faced with actions which they find shocking and unintelligible, the surviving characters seek, with a haste that is almost indecent, to put them out of sight and out of mind. Their reaction is that of the normal ordinary man, and, as such, serves to underline for the last time the remoteness of Othello from those among whom he has lived and moved. The most immediately and impressively heroic of all the tragic heroes is granted no epic valediction from the mouths of others, no ceremonious rites of funeral; primarily, of course, because he has forfeited all claim to them through his crime in murdering Desdemona, but also, I think, because he is, and always has been, a mystery and a challenge to the unheroic world in which fate and circumstance have placed him. His relationship to that world, and his isolation from it, are both stated in the final couplet. The Venetian state must be acquainted with the death of its greatest soldier and servant; but there is no indication that it will, in any real sense, be seriously affected by that death. Bradley is surely right when he says of Othello:

his deed and his death have not that influence on the interests of a nation or an empire which serve to idealise, and to remove far from our own sphere, the stories of Hamlet and Macbeth, of Coriolanus and Antony. Indeed he is already superseded at Cyprus when his fate is consummated, and as we leave him no vision rises on us, as in the other tragedies, of peace descending on a distracted land.[1]

The unusual nature of the ending points directly, as Bradley indicates, to the unusual nature of the entire play when seen in the context of Shakespearian tragedy in general. The characteristic pattern of all the other tragedies is an expanding one. Whether the action takes its rise out of a specific act by an individual—Claudius's poisoning of Hamlet's father, and Lear's giving away of his kingdom, for example—or out of the response by a character to some new situation with which he is confronted, as Brutus is by the offering of a crown to Caesar, or Macbeth by his encounter with the witches, it tends to spread and to widen its scope. The initial event that triggers it off is like a stone thrown into the middle of a pond. A turbulence is set up, which rapidly extends to affect a city, a country, an empire, and, in some cases, even the elements.

Romeo and Juliet, so often regarded as an immature tragedy, conforms to this generalization. Coming into conflict with the feud between Montagues and Capulets, the relationship of the lovers leads to the death of Mercutio, thus involving the Prince far more deeply and intimately in the struggle than he has been hitherto, and to the deaths of Tybalt and Paris, as well as those of the hero and heroine. Moreover, it also has an effect on the state, since it ultimately results in the reconciliation of the warring families. There is something of the history play about *Romeo and Juliet*; and, in this respect, it looks forward to all the tragedies that were to follow, with the single exception of *Othello*, which, significantly, came to exercise a powerful influence on later Jacobean and Caroline drama at precisely the time when playwrights ceased to concern themselves with the dramatization of large public themes and issues. Of all Shakepeare's tragedies it was *Othello* that left the deepest mark on the art of John Ford.

The unique quality of Shakespearian tragedy in general, distinguishing it from all other tragedy written at the time, is due in no small measure, it seems to me, to the fact that Shakespeare came to tragedy by way of the history play. It was through the continuous exploration of historical matter that he discovered and penetrated into the intimate connexions between the private decision and its public consequences, between the political action and its repercussions on the individual psyche. It is this unremitting two-way traffic between the private and the public worlds that, more perhaps than anything else, gives his tragedies that density of experience and that closeness to life which sets them apart from the tragedies of his contemporaries. Brutus and Macbeth feel and undergo in themselves, at the moment of temptation, the conflict and the dissension that the decision they are about to take will bring upon their countries.

It is exactly this close interconnexion of the public and the private that is not present in *Othello*— at least not in its usual form—though this fact is by no means evident at the play's opening. In Act I the imminence of a Turkish attack on Cyprus and preparations for the defence of the island demand as much attention from the audience as the marriage of Othello and Desdemona, on which they have a considerable impact, or as Iago's gulling of Roderigo. Indeed, the first spectators to see the play must have thought, up to the beginning of Act II, that they were about to witness an action in which the struggle for the control of the eastern Mediterranean that culminated in the battle of Lepanto would be a leading, if not a central, theme. Shakespeare was touching on more recent history than any he had handled hitherto and on events that had affected the whole of Christendom. Moreover, at the time when he was writing his play the long conflict between Turks and Christians had just received a most impressive formulation in English at the hands of Richard Knolles, whose *The Generall Historie of the Turkes* was first published in 1603 and excited so much interest that four further editions were to be called for in the next thirty-five years.[2] More than one spectator in 1604 may well have experienced a sense of disappointment on hearing the announcement 'News, lads! our wars are done' (II, i, 20), since it could only mean that the Turkish capture of Cyprus and the brutal murder of the Venetian commander of Famagusta, Marco Antonio Bragadino, in 1571, were not, after all, to have their place in the story.

But before Act II begins there have already been indications of the direction in which the action is moving. One of the most striking features of Act I is the frequency with which public affairs of the utmost consequence give way in it to private matters. The third scene opens with the Venetian Senate hurriedly gathered together at night for an extraordinary meeting in order to decide what measures are to be taken to counter the imminent invasion of Cyprus. Yet, despite the extreme urgency of the business, they break off their deliberations to listen, first to Brabantio's complaint against Othello, then to the Moor's defence of himself and his actions, and finally to Desdemona's assertion of her love for him. Only after all this has happened does the Duke invest Othello with the supreme command in Cyprus; and no sooner has Othello accepted this office than the discussion in the Senate turns to the question of whether his wife shall accompany him or not. The incongruous nature of the entire proceedings did not escape the sharp eye and censorious judgement of Thomas Rymer, who expressed his scepticism and disapproval with a vigorous display of that derisive buffoonery which came so easily to him. He writes:

So, by and by, we find the Duke of Venice, with his Senators in Councel, at Midnight, upon advice that the Turks, or Ottamites, or both together, were ready in transport Ships, put to Sea, in order to make a Descent upon *Cyprus*. This is the posture when we see *Brabantio* and *Othello* join them. By their Conduct and manner of talk, a body must strain hard to fancy the Scene at *Venice*; And not rather in some of our Cinq-ports, where the Baily and his Fisher-men are knocking their heads together on account of some Whale, or some terrible broil upon the Coast. But to shew them true Venetians, the Maritime affairs stick not long on their hand; the publick may sink or swim. They will sit up all night to hear a Doctors Commons, Matrimonial Cause: and have the merits of the Cause at large laid open to 'em, that they may decide it before they Stir.3

Acting in his customary capacity of counsel for the prosecution, Rymer, the lawyer and historian, has made a point that more recent criticism of the play has tended to ignore: by all normal standards of behaviour the actions of the Venetian Senate are highly improbable. Yet they are clearly an essential part of Shakespeare's design, since there is no counterpart to them in the story he was drawing on. The wars between Venice and the Turks have no place in Cinthio's narrative. There Othello merely goes to Cyprus in the regular course of duty as the replacement for a governor whose term of office has expired, not as the man who is best fitted to cope with a great crisis. The setting provided by the momentous affairs of 1571, which meant so much more to an audience in 1604 than they do to an audience today, is something added by Shakespeare to his source for sound dramatic reasons. Improbable though the scene in the Senate may appear when viewed in isolation, it works superbly well within the context of the play, where it has a complex function. It establishes the superior worth and dignity of the hero over those whom he serves; he is the indispensable man in complete control of an ugly situation. It brings out the total devotion of Desdemona to him, since she is prepared to face not only her father's displeasure but also the hazards of war in order to be with the man of her choice. And it leaves the audience with at least a suspicion that, were it not for the military crisis, the attitude of the Duke and the Senate towards the marriage might well be rather different. Rymer is wrong when he says that so far as the Senate is concerned 'the publick may sink or swim'; the point of the scene is that they can see no hope for the state except in Othello.

Once public matters have fulfilled this purpose of helping to define the supreme importance and value of the hero, and of establishing the depth of the love that exists between him and Desdemona, they are dismissed as quickly as possible. They receive their quietus in the brief scene (II, ii) which is given over to Herald's proclamation that the wars are done and that the night is to be devoted to general rejoicing. The last echo of the initial political situation is heard in II, iii, when Othello, faced with the brawl engineered by Iago, speaks of the nameless seaport as 'a town of war, / Yet wild, the people's hearts brimful of fear'. But this is the first and the last that we ever hear about the people of Cyprus and their state of mind. They appear only once; they say nothing; they do not matter. The course of the action affects them no more than they affect it. In III, ii Othello sends news to the Venetian Senate, and then goes off to view a fortification. It is his final act as a military commander. From this point onwards public affairs are not mentioned at all again until III, iv, when Desdemona, at a loss to account for Othello's unwonted behaviour to her, invokes them, quite mistakenly, as a possible excuse and explanation, saying to Emilia:

> Something sure of state
> Either from Venice, or some unhatch'd practice
> Made demonstrable here in Cyprus to him,
> Hath puddled his clear spirit...

By this time, however, 'Othello's occupation's gone'; the outer world of military activity and political decision, in which he once moved with such calm assurance and which was his natural sphere, has ceased to exist for him in its own right. When Lodovico arrives in Cyprus towards the end of IV, i, bringing the letters announcing that Cassio is to become governor of the island, Othello receives them with the dignified submission of the great public servant, saying:

> I kiss the instrument of their pleasures.

But the news itself means nothing to him. His reading of the letters is a mere pretence to cover the avid and unworthy curiosity with which he eavesdrops on the innocent conversation of Desdemona and her kinsman on the subject of Cassio—a conversation that confirms all his worst suspicions and drives him to the outrageous action of striking his wife. Obsessed by the one consuming passion of jealousy, he can no longer see anything as in itself it really is, otherwise he would realize that if Desdemona were in love with Cassio she would not express joy at hearing news that must mean her separation from him. As it is, however, he draws the words and actions of others into the private nightmare world of confusion and uncertainty in which he now lives, and there they undergo a hideous distortion. Instead of being, like the other tragedies, a play of expansion, *Othello* is a play of contraction. The action does not widen out, it narrows down as public business is increasingly excluded from it until it finds its catastrophe, not on the battle-field, nor in the presence of a court, but in a bedroom at night where two people, united by the closest of ties, speak at cross purposes and misunderstand each other disastrously, with no thought of turning to the independent witness, Emilia, who could reveal the truth and save both of them. Indeed, Othello has taken care to ensure that Emilia shall not be present. The pattern of this tragedy is that of a whirlpool, with its centre in the poisoned mind of the hero which reshapes, distorts, and degrades objective reality. At the heart of *Othello* there is a kind of darkness. Only Iago knows what is true and what is false, and he does his best to confuse the distinction between them in his own mind as well as in the minds of others. Misled and misinformed by him, the rest of the characters misinterpret the events in which they are caught up. Alone of

Shakespeare's tragic heroes Othello does not even know who his true antagonist is until the play is within fewer than a hundred and fifty lines of its conclusion.

This radical difference in the tragic pattern is demanded because *Othello*, it seems to me, embodies and defines another sort of tragic experience from that which is to be found in the rest of the tragedies. In them the conflict in which the protagonist is involved and which he may have been largely responsible for causing, as Brutus, Lear, Coriolanus, and, above all, Macbeth have been, becomes an open one by the end of Act III at the latest. By this stage too it has assumed political dimensions. Even in *Romeo and Juliet* Romeo is banished on the Prince's orders in order to prevent further strife. Having taken on these proportions, the conflict then leads not only to the death of the hero but also to the destruction of some great potential for good—the idealistic hopes of Brutus, the princely promise of Hamlet, the innate nobility of Macbeth. Furthermore, in the course of this conflict, a whole system of values and a way of life are either threatened with destruction or even swept away. At the end of it all, it is true, some positive force, some new kind of order, emerges out of the wreckage; but it is the destructive process that fills the imagination, and that which survives seems an inadequate substitute for that which has been lost. In *Othello*, however, it is not a great potentiality for good that is destroyed but rather something of transcendent value that has actually been realized and made concrete during the course of the play. The love of the Moor and Desdemona is triumphantly rendered through the action and the poetry of the first four scenes. In spite of, or even because of, Iago's denigrations of it, it is this love that dominates the opening which celebrates its achievement. One's awareness of it and admiration for it rise in a crescendo to reach their culmination in the rhapsodic reunion scene, II, i, where Othello voices his sense of its surpassing excellence by saying:

> If it were now to die,
> 'Twere now to be most happy; for I fear
> My soul hath her content so absolute
> That not another comfort like to this
> Succeeds in unknown fate.

The happiness is so intense as to be almost unbearable. Yet this happiness is destroyed so completely that at the end of the play one has no sense of any part of it, no matter how small or inadequate, continuing. The ruin is total. Nothing remains of the music of concord that Othello and Desdemona once made together except the poignant memory of its sweetness and its beauty.

Othello is about the wanton destruction of happiness—something so precious and so fragile that its loss is felt as quite irredeemable. This, I think, is the fundamental source of the peculiar sense of pain and anguish that this tragedy, more than any of the others, leaves in the consciousness of a spectator or a reader. But there are two other related features of the play which add to and sharpen the pain. The relationship of the hero and the heroine is—and one of the miracles of *Othello* is the unobtrusive artistry with which Shakespeare produces this effect—a thing of rare and extraordinary beauty. Warm, moving, and vital, it has at the same time some of the qualities of an artifact. The mutual passion of Romeo and Juliet is spontaneous and instinctive; that of Antony and Cleopatra is the fruit of knowledge and experience—there has been an element of deliberate calculation on both sides. But the love of Othello and Desdemona is something that has grown gradually, then been discovered intuitively, then fashioned consciously,

71

and, finally, achieved by them in the face of all the obstacles to it set up by their differences of race and colour, their disparity in years, and the opposition to it of the society to which they belong. Drawn by the fascination of Othello's story of his life into the strange, remote, heroic world which he inhabits, Desdemona has become part of that world, which is itself a work of art created by the hero out of his own experience. Listening to the Moor, as he relates his history to the Senate and re-enacts the drama of his wooing, one is aware of the story as a romantic epic of love and war. There is also a trace of the myth of Pygmalion and Galatea about it all as Othello, first unconsciously, then with a growing awareness of what he is doing, converts the 'maiden never bold, / Of spirit so still and quiet that her motion / Blush'd at herself' into his 'fair warrior', ready to make a 'storm of fortunes', to defy her father and public opinion, and to avow her love in the Senate. And just as Othello has, in part at least, created the Desdemona that he loves, actualizing possibilities within her that have hitherto lain dormant, so she, in her love for him, has, as it were, completed him by recognizing in him a beauty invisible to other eyes yet indubitably there. It is Desdemona who gives the finishing touch to the poem that Othello has made of his life when she says:

> I saw Othello's visage in his mind;
> And to his honours and his valiant parts
> Did I my soul and fortunes consecrate.

It is not only the value of what is destroyed in *Othello* that gives pain, but also the sheer loveliness and perfection of what is destroyed. To a far greater extent than in any other of the tragedies the aesthetic sense is directly involved in and affected by the tragic experience that the play provides.

The distinctive feature of the destructive process in *Othello* is its ugliness, for what the hero is subjected to is a deliberate and calculated degradation such as no other of Shakespeare's tragic heroes undergoes. Hamlet is partially corrupted by the corrupt world in which he finds himself, but no one sets out to corrupt him. Macbeth degenerates, but this is a consequence of his own actions. Lear and Gloucester suffer horrible and degrading cruelty at the hands of their antagonists, but the main end those antagonists have in view is their own material advancement. In *Othello*, however, the urge that impels Iago to his intrigues is no desire for political or military power, not even primarily the desire for gain, but an absolute need to denigrate and undermine all that is true, good, and beautiful. His first reason for seeking Cassio's death is because, as he explains in v, i,

> He hath a daily beauty in his life
> That makes me ugly.

The daily life of Othello and Desdemona is infinitely more beautiful than that of Cassio; and the impulse Iago feels to desecrate that beauty is, therefore, correspondingly stronger. It speaks out unequivocally in the opening scene through the coarse and brutal imagery which he employs to describe the union of the lovers. After that first scene there is no need to look for further motives. What D. H. Lawrence calls 'the desire to do dirt on life' is common enough; it is only the intensity with which Iago feels this compulsion that is unusual. As the driving force for a tragic action, however, this hatred of the spiritual and the ideal is without a parallel, so far as I am aware, in the whole range of Elizabethan drama, though the unremitting malice with which the Aragonian brothers ruin their sister's happiness in *The Duchess of Malfi* looks like a partial imita-

72

tion of it. If it is, Webster's handling of the matter only serves to point up that which is unique in Shakespeare's. Ferdinand and the Cardinal never succeeded in imposing their warped vision of life on the Duchess as Iago does succeed for a time in imposing his on Othello; and, as a consequence, there is no scene in *The Duchess of Malfi*, despite Webster's fondness for the sensational and the macabre, that is anything like so shocking or painful as that in which Othello strikes Desdemona (IV, i) or that in which he treats her as though she were a whore in a brothel (IV, ii). In both these scenes it is the unmerited suffering of the heroine that causes the immediate distress that Bradley noted, but within the total experience of the play it is the evidence they afford of the degradation Othello has undergone that matters even more, and it is precisely this that Shakespeare draws attention to. Towards the end of IV, i, Lodovico, the dispassionate spectator, expresses his amazement at the change that has taken place in Othello by saying:

> Is this the noble Moor whom our full Senate
> Call all in all sufficient? Is this the nature
> Whom passion could not shake, whose solid virtue
> The shot of accident nor dart of chance
> Could neither graze nor pierce?

The events that follow make Lodovico's questions even more cogent, but the final answer the play gives to them is an emphatic yes, for, terrible and harrowing though the degradation of Othello is, it is not complete. The Moor's speech before he stabs himself is not, as T. S. Eliot suggested, an attempt at cheering himself up. It is rather the ultimate defeat of Iago, for it shows that the Ancient has not, after all, ensnared the hero's soul. Enough of the servant of the Venetian republic survives to enable Othello to reaffirm the values by which he once lived and to execute justice on himself. Unlike the other tragic heroes, he speaks his own valediction. He has to, because he is the only character left, now that Desdemona is dead, who is fitted and qualified to do so. The unusual ending of this tragedy is dictated by its unusual nature.

© G. R. HIBBARD 1968

NOTES

1. A. C. Bradley, *Shakespearean Tragedy* (1957 edition), p. 146.

2. I find it difficult to believe that Shakespeare had not been reading Knolles at the time he was writing *Othello*. The references to the size of the Turkish fleet and to the meeting of two fleets off Rhodes (I, iii, 1–39) look like reminiscences of the three passages from *The Generall Historie of the Turkes* (4th edition, 1631) that follow. (*a*) 'About the middle of April following he [Selymus] sent *Piall Bassa* with fourescore gallies and thirty galliots to keepe the Venetians from sending aid into Cyprus' (p. 845 E). (*b*) After attempting to take the island of Tenos, the Turks 'shamefully gaue ouer the assault, and abandoning the Island, directed their course toward Cyprus. For *Mustapha* authour of that expedition (for his antient hatred against the Christians made Generall by *Selymus*) had before appointed *Piall Bassa* at a time prefixed to meet him at the Rhodes, and that he that came first should tarrie for the other, that so they might together sayle into Cyprus' (p. 846 G). (*c*) 'he [Mustapha] together with *Haly Bassa* and the rest of the fleet departed from Constantinople the six and twentieth of May, and at the Rhodes met with *Piall*, as he had before appointed. The whole fleet at that time consisted of two hundred gallies, amongst whom were diuers galliots, and small

men of war, with diuers other vessels prepared for the transportation of horses: with this fleet *Mustapha* kept on his course for Cyprus' (p. 846L).

It is also possible, I think, that the unusual name Ragozine in *Measure for Measure* (IV, iii, 67) may have been suggested to Shakespeare by Knolles's mention of two people called Ragazonius. The first, Hieronimus Ragazonius, was the Bishop of Famagusta at the time of the Turkish invasion (p. 855B), and was sent to Venice to warn the Senate about 'the dangerous estate of the citie, the strength of the enemie, the weakenes of the defendants against so great a Multitude' (p. 855C). The other, Iacobus Ragazonius, was sent to Constantinople by the Venetians to make a treaty with the Turks (p. 857D).

3. Thomas Rymer, *A Short View of Tragedy* (1693). Quoted from *Critical Essays of the Seventeenth Century*, ed. J. E. Spingarn (1908), II, 227–8.

THE TWO PARTS OF *OTHELLO*

BY

NED B. ALLEN

I

In this paper I wish to examine the composition of *Othello*. The best place to start would seem to me to be Shakespeare's source.[1]

In my first section, Cinthio's tale, the third tale of the seventh decade of his *Hecatommithi*, will be examined, and a new attempt will be made to ascertain how it influenced *Othello*. This study of the relationship between one of the most prosaic of Shakespeare's sources and one of the most poetic of his tragedies will, it is hoped, throw light on his creative process. For this purpose *Othello* is better than *Julius Caesar* or even *Richard II*, especially in view of the fact that its structure is usually praised beyond that of any other Shakespearian play.

The story of the Moor of Venice is a kind of exemplum. The tales of Cinthio's third decade originally, it is obvious, were all intended to be about disloyal husbands and wives, and the preceding tale, mentioned in the head-link, concerns a dissolute, adulterous wife justly killed by her husband. Curtio, who tells the story of the Moor, prefers not to be so erotic as the other narrators, whose pretence of preaching morality is usually little more than an excuse for dwelling on salacious adventures, and he therefore, here and in his later tales, describes chaste rather than adulterous characters.[2] Here his purpose is to show that not all women are unchaste and not all jealous husbands are justified in their suspicions. Like many of the other narrators, Curtio describes his characters effectively. It is not true, as has so often been asserted, that they are mere hooks on which to hang the plot. Cinthio's Disdemona, his Moor, and his Alfiero might all be considered well drawn if they were not so far outshone by their parallels in Shakespeare's drama.

Shakespeare is much closer to his source in some parts of the play than in others. Acts I and II owe comparatively little to Cinthio and almost bear out the claim of some critics that Shakespeare took only the bare outlines of his plot from him.

In the first scene Iago's assurance to Roderigo that he hates the Moor and the reason he gives for it—that Othello has promoted Cassio above him—is not even hinted at by Cinthio, who represents the Alfiero as plotting largely against Disdemona, not her husband,[3] and the profane rousing of Brabantio is likewise Shakespeare's own. There is, of course, no Brabantio in Cinthio, and no Roderigo. Cinthio's influence is comparatively absent, too, from the rest of Act I. Beyond telling us that the Moor and Disdemona married against the wishes of her family, that the Senate sent the Moor to Cyprus, and that Disdemona showed her love for her husband by insisting that she be allowed to accompany him there, Cinthio has little that has influenced Shakespeare. The story of Othello's wooing of Desdemona—or rather her wooing of him—is all Shakespeare's, and the dramatically effective crisis caused by the Turkish attack on Cyprus is also his. Cinthio says merely that the Senate made a routine change when they sent the Moor to Cyprus.

Not until Iago's soliloquy at the end of I, iii, do we find further use of Cinthio. There Iago outlines his plan—to arouse Othello's jealousy by persuading him that Cassio is 'too familiar with his wife.' This is clearly suggested by Cinthio's: 'And, turning over in his mind various plans to this end—all wicked and villainous—he decided that he would accuse her of adultery to her husband and give him to understand that the adulterer was the *Capo di squadra*' (*Et riuolgendosi per l'animo uarie cose, tutte scelerate & maluagie, alla fine deliberò di uoluerla accusare di Adulterio al marito, & dargli ad intendere, che l'Adultero era il Capo di squadra*). Iago's two soliloquies in Act II—with which Shakespeare closes scenes i and iii—were likewise suggested, of course, by this line in Cinthio. The soliloquy at the end of II, i also reveals Cinthio's influence in Iago's thereafter-forgotten assertion: 'Now I do love her too.' Though Shakespeare makes no further reference to this declaration, it was obviously suggested by Cinthio's statement that the Alfiero fell most ardently in love with Disdemona (*s'innamorò di Disdemona ardentissimamente*).

Even these three soliloquies are largely made up of ideas not found in Cinthio: Iago's 'justification' of his plans by voicing his suspicion that both Othello and Cassio have cuckolded him, his repeated likening of Othello to an ass, and his admission that his plan is a devilish one. And the remainder of Acts I and II is also largely made up of similar additions to and enlargements on the bare outline furnished by Cinthio. Cinthio says nothing about the arrival in Cyprus or about the events of the first night there.

With Act III, however, Shakespeare's attitude toward his source seems to change. After a scene in which he again represents Iago as directing his plot in a way not suggested by Cinthio—by helping Cassio make his application to Desdemona—and another very short scene to be discussed later, Shakespeare begins with III, iii to follow the novella as closely as he has followed any source. Instead of enlarging on the bare outlines of Cinthio, instead of improvising and digressing as he has in the first two acts, Shakespeare here shows such respect for the details of the source that he leaves out scarcely any of them. He makes the language of the characters poetic, and that, of course, involves changes, but much of *Othello*, beginning with III, iii, is as close to Cinthio as *Julius Caesar* and *Antony and Cleopatra* are to North's Plutarch. The occasion of Iago's first hint that Desdemona and Cassio are guilty, his pretended reluctance to speak further, his protestations about the love and duty which he owes Othello, his claim that 'our country disposition'—that of Venetian women—is to deceive husbands, his suggestion that there is something unnatural in her loving a black man, his further pretence that he dislikes to incriminate others, Othello's painful reactions and his threatening demand for further proof, and Iago's use of the handkerchief (though he gets hold of it in a manner very different from that in the source) are all very close to Cinthio. Nearly all of Shakespeare's most striking verbal reminiscences of Cinthio are in this part of the play.

Moreover, this respect for the source continues through most of the last three acts of the tragedy. Though Shakespeare introduces many new things—the scene in which Othello treats Desdemona like a prostitute (IV, i), the substitution of Bianca for Cassio's female servant, the use of Roderigo, and, of course, the magnificent transformation of the catastrophe which results from Shakespeare's new way of ending the lives of Desdemona and Othello—in spite of all these dramatically effective improvements, it must still be observed that the latter part of the play is close to Cinthio, and *much* closer than Acts I and II. Othello's demands for the handkerchief from Desdemona (III, iv), Iago's claim that Cassio has boasted of his conquest of Desdemona (IV, i, 25–9), his conversation with Cassio about Bianca which Othello is allowed to see but not to overhear (IV, i, 103 ff.), his sight of the handkerchief in Bianca's possession (IV, i, 158),[4] Desdemona's plea for help from Emilia and Iago,[5] and the attempt on Cassio's life (except for Roderigo's part in it) are all from Cinthio. Even the words of Desdemona when she learns from Othello that she is to die: 'Then Lord have mercy on me', are an echo of the last words of Cinthio's heroine. He tells us that she died 'calling on God for aid' (*chiamando Iddio che l'aiutasse*).

II

One wonders what caused this change in Shakespeare's attitude toward Cinthio. Why did he have so much more respect for his ideas in the latter part of the play than in Acts I and II?

Upon a careful comparison, one finds other differences between what may be called the two parts of *Othello*. There is a difference in atmosphere, a difference in movement like that in two movements of a symphony. In the first part—Acts I and II—the action takes place evenly, normally, as it seems to in our every day lives. In the last three acts it moves with horrifying speed, so that a trustful husband becomes in a short time a jealous, murderous one, and then, as the tempo increases, becomes even more suddenly a loving husband again and a suicide.

This change in movement, with its crescendo in the second part, must have been observed by nearly every reader and theatregoer,[6] and other differences between the two parts of the play are even more obvious. Note the contradictions between them observable in the character of Cassio and what he does. In the first part he is 'almost damned in a fair wife' (I, i, 21); in the latter part he is a bachelor. When he hears in I, ii, 52 that Othello is married, he asks, 'To who?' but in III, iii, 71 and 100, Desdemona and Othello both say that he came awooing with Othello and went between them very oft.[7] In the first part he gets drunk and wounds Montano so severely that Montano is 'hurt to danger' (II, iii, 197); yet in the latter part, twenty-four hours later when the two men meet in the fatal bedchamber, Montano seems to be in perfect health, strong enough to disarm Othello, and not in the least antagonistic to Cassio (V, ii, 235–82). Moreover, though Cassio feels in II, iii that his drunkenness was the greatest part of his fault and says:

I will ask him for my place again: he shall tell me I am a drunkard, (306–7)

he never mentions the drinking incident in the latter part, nor do any of the other characters, not even Iago. In Act II, the principal characters in the tragedy are all interested in their delivery from the Turkish attack and in the celebration of Othello's and Desdemona's marriage; but on the next day—throughout the rest of the drama—they make no reference to the Turks (though Othello has come to Cyprus solely to repel them), nor to the marriage as a recent event. In Acts I and II Iago explains—to Roderigo and in soliloquy—his motives for revenge against Othello and Cassio, but in Acts III, IV, and V he never refers, even elliptically, to any of them. Most surprisingly of all, Othello and Desdemona do not in Acts III, IV, and V act like a newly married couple. This leads us to another dissimilarity between the two parts of *Othello*—the two time schemes of the action.

It has often been observed that in this play Shakespeare is not consistent in his treatment of time—that on some occasions Othello's marriage is represented as having just been consummated, while on others he seems to have been married for weeks or months. Though ridiculed by Rymer, and still considered a flaw by Daniel, Fleay, Bradley, and others,[8] this Double Time is by most critics held to be one of the greatest proofs of Shakespeare's extraordinary ability as a dramatist. In 1850 John Wilson first claimed that the contradictions in the time schedule of *Othello* showed Shakespeare's skill rather than his carelessness.[9] He declared that Shakespeare subtly used a short time schedule to maintain the tension of passion and a long time schedule to make Iago's stories credible. Most twentieth-century critics, including the Shakespeare sceptics, have been willing to let this mid-nineteenth-century altar to Shakespeare's art remain virtually untouched, and the editors of the latest editions of *Othello* still bow before it.[10] Even Stoll, the least worshipful of the twentieth-century Shakespeare scholars, calls the Double Time in *Othello* an example of Shakespeare's 'nobler opportunism' and adds that the two time schedules conspired 'happily' together on Shakespeare's stage.[11] The very fact that 'Double Time' is usually capitalized indicates the attitude of most critics.

No one seems to have noticed the significance of the fact that the double time in *Othello* is not scattered throughout the play—that the two times exist separately, one in Acts I and II, and the other in the rest of the play. The double time is, therefore, one of the contrasting features of the two parts of *Othello*.[12] Consider the following.

The first two acts of *Othello* take place in an easily measured space of time beginning with the marriage of Othello and Desdemona in Venice and ending with the consummation of this marriage in Cyprus, at which time Cassio gets drunk and is cashiered by Othello. We are not sure just how long the voyage from Venice to Cyprus lasts, and time does pass very quickly between the sighting of the ships carrying Desdemona and Othello and their landings, but here there is no other time sequence to confuse us.[13] Beginning with Act III, however, we find another time plan. Othello and Desdemona have been married for some weeks or months. Cassio has just lost his place, and Desdemona's efforts to persuade Othello to restore it to him, Iago's ensnaring of Othello's soul and Desdemona's, Emilia's and Othello's deaths all take place in one day. Moreover, *all* the references to a longer time can be explained if we assume that when he wrote this part of the play Shakespeare thought of all the characters, not as having arrived in Cyprus on the previous day, but as having long been there—as in Cinthio.

During this part of the action there are almost no specific references to the events of Acts I and II. Iago speaks of Desdemona's father—'She did deceive her father marrying you' and 'He thought 'twas witchcraft'—but we hear nothing about any of the other things Shakespeare added to Cinthio in the earlier part, about the wedding celebration on Cyprus, about Cassio's drunkenness, or any of the details of his fault. And *everything* from here on points to, or at least agrees with, the supposition that when he wrote Acts III, IV, and V Shakespeare was thinking of Othello's marriage as an event of the past—just as Cinthio had at this point in the plot.

It is obvious that these many contradictions are not to be explained lightly as momentary carelessness on Shakespeare's part. There are too many of them. Moreover, the fact that they are distributed, not haphazardly, but in such a way as to divide the drama into two parts seems to be significant and must be taken into consideration. This is most strikingly true of the double time, which does not appear to be a subtly contrived device created to achieve a complicated and varying impact on the theatregoers, but a simple shift from one time to another.[14] And every one of the contradictions mentioned is a contradiction of something in the first part of the play with something in the latter part. It is surprising, in fact, to find that there are scarcely any contradictions within either of the two parts—that if we read the first two and the last three acts as separate units we find each of them as carefully integrated, as well knit, as any of the other plays.[15]

How can the discrepancies between these two well-unified parts of *Othello* be explained?

<h1 style="text-align:center">III</h1>

It seems certain that Shakespeare wrote the two parts of *Othello* at different times—in different frames of mind—and that the double time—like the other contradictions between the two parts—is the result of his having joined them carelessly. We have a great deal of evidence that Shakespeare was careless about details. He no doubt realized that his audience would not be likely to notice anything wrong, and he apparently thought of the play as something to be acted only a few times before being replaced by something else. He probably never dreamed that scholars would be studying *Othello* in the twentieth century, and if he had been told that his splicing of disparate bits of his treatment of the Moor of Venice would one day be called a miracle of subtle planning, he would surely have called the whole idea an improbable fiction.

Though the thesis here presented is merely that the two parts of *Othello* were written at different times, or at least in different frames of mind, it seems most likely—for reasons to be explained later—that Shakespeare wrote the second part first. Poe advises short-story writers to proceed in this way, and the method has some advantages. Let us consider the latter part of *Othello* first.

At the beginning of Act III, Cassio is asking the musicians to play for the General. He says nothing about Othello's having been recently married, nor does the Clown who asks the musicians to go away. When Cassio speaks to Iago later in the scene, we learn that Cassio has been up all night. We discover that he has been guilty of some fault and that as a result he has lost his place, but neither he nor anyone else says anything about its having been committed on the first night Othello and Desdemona spent together, nor do they mention the voyage from Venice or Cassio's drunkenness. Emilia tells Cassio:

He you hurt is of great fame in Cyprus,   (III, i, 48)

and it seems likely that when he wrote this line Shakespeare had not made up his mind to have the fault any other than the one indicated in the source, where Cinthio says that the *Capo di squadra* was dismissed 'because while on guard had drawn his sword against a soldier and had wounded him' (*per hauer messo mano alla spada...nella guardia contra un soldato & dategli delle ferite*). It is significant that Montano, with whom we who have just read Acts I and II are well acquainted, is not mentioned by name, and that *all* subsequent references to Cassio's fault are general. In III, iv, 115 he speaks of it merely as 'my offence'.

As we have noted, Acts III and IV are much closer to the source than are Acts I and II. Iago's arguments follow the arguments of the Alfiero in Cinthio, and we can well suppose that when Shakespeare wrote this part of the play he had not yet decided just what Cassio's fault would be, and he had not yet decided to make Othello's marriage a recent event. He was following Cinthio, who represents Othello as having been married for some time before his jealousy is aroused.

In III, iii Othello has none of the characteristics of a newlywed,[16] nor does Desdemona when she enters at the opening of III, iii. She mentions Cassio's 'cause', but, like Emilia earlier, she does not refer to Montano, nor does she say anything to indicate that Shakespeare thought of representing Cassio as having been drunk on their wedding night when he wrote the lines.[17] And there is *no* indication that they have just arrived in Cyprus. Everything, indeed, agrees with the supposition that when Shakespeare wrote this part of the drama he was representing the characters, not as having recently experienced the events of Acts I and II, but as having lived in Cyprus for a long time.

All the indications of double time in Act III are explained by this supposition. It explains Emilia's statement about the handkerchief:

> My wayward husband hath a hundred times
> Wooed me to steal it. (III, iii, 292–3)

It explains Othello's statements:

> I slept the next night well, was free and merry
> I found not Cassio's kisses on her lips. (III, iii, 340–1)

> I had been happy if the general camp
> Pioneers and all had tasted her sweet body
> So I had nothing known. (III, iii, 345–7)

It explains Iago's words:

> I lay with Cassio lately... (III, iii, 413)

> Have you not sometimes seen a handkerchief
> Spotted with strawberries in your wife's hand? (III, iii, 434–5)

It explains Emilia's statement:

> 'Tis not a year or two shows us a man. (III, iv, 105)

It explains Desdemona's defence of the male sex:

> Nay we must think men are not gods,
> Nor of them look for such observancy
> As fits the bridal. (III, iv, 148–50)

Desdemona surely implies here that her own bridal is an event of the past. And her lament:

> Alas the day, I never gave him cause (III, iv, 162)

is in complete harmony with this. Obviously, Desdemona and Othello in the last three acts of the play are not newlyweds. It explains Bianca's charge:

> What, keep a week away? seven days and nights? (III, iv, 173)

and her claim:

> This is some token from a newer friend. (III, iv, 181)

The rest of the play (Acts IV and V) is in perfect harmony with the time scheme of Act III. The supposition that Shakespeare *always* in the last three acts of the drama thought of Othello and Desdemona as long married and long resident in Cyprus is supported again and again. It explains why Cassio accepts Iago's lie:

> My lord is fallen into an epilepsy.
> This is his second fit; he had one yesterday.   (IV, i, 51–2)

It is especially necessary to explain Lodovico's coming from Venice with orders for Othello's return (IV, i, 228–48). Such a decision might have been delivered after intervals of various lengths, but not on the day after Othello's arrival in Cyprus, for we must surely suppose that it would take much longer for the Senate to hear of the passing of the Turkish threat, for them to make their decision, and for Lodovico to sail with this decision to Cyprus. It explains Iago's pretence that he has *often* seen Othello strike Desdemona (IV, i, 288–9). It explains Othello's questions to Emilia and her replies:

> *Othello:* You have seen nothing then?
> *Emilia:* Nor ever heard, nor ever did suspect.
>
> . . . .
>
> *Othello:* What, did they never whisper?
> *Emilia:*   Never, my Lord.
>   (IV, ii, 1–2 and 6)

It explains Desdemona's words:

>   I never did
> Offend you in my life, never loved Cassio
> But with such general warranty of Heaven
> As I might love. I never gave him token.   (V, ii, 58–61)

It explains Desdemona's request to Emilia:

>   Prithee tonight
> Lay on my bed my wedding sheets.   (IV, ii, 105–6)

It explains Iago's words to Emilia:

> What, are you mad? I charge you, get you home.   (V, ii, 194)

In Cinthio, of course, the Alfiero's wife is not a servant. She lives with the Alfiero in a home of their own. This reference to that home, besides indicating that Shakespeare thought of them as having lived in Cyprus long enough to have acquired a residence, also reveals the close relationship of this part of the drama to Cinthio.

Most important in the present discussion are Othello's words:

> 'Tis pitiful, but yet Iago knows
> That she with Cassio hath the act of shame
> A thousand times committed.   (V, ii, 210–12)

This last is, of course, according to any time scheme, an angry exaggeration, but it agrees with the other proofs that Shakespeare *always* while he was writing the last three acts of the play made all the characters speak as if a long time had elapsed since the marriage.[18]

As has been said, it seems most probable that, after having written the last three acts of *Othello*, Shakespeare then turned to Acts I and II. And he seems to have had a new outlook. Possibly some time had elapsed. Perhaps the fact that dramatic necessity had forced him to depart from Cinthio at the end made him feel like departing even further from him in the exposition. At any rate, he made much greater changes in Cinthio there than he had made in Acts III and IV. He also gave Cassio a wife (in one line, at least), pictured Iago's wickedness as stemming in part from anger because Cassio has been given the place he wanted and in part from a suspicion that both Othello and Cassio have cuckolded him, and he represented Cassio's fault as taking place on the night of the arrival of all the chief characters in Cyprus, the night of the consummation of Othello's marriage.

It may be argued, of course, that there is no way of being sure that the latter part of *Othello* was written first. All that is indicated by the discrepancies between the two parts is that Shakespeare wrote them at different times and in different moods. But it seems more likely that he started with Act III. According to this thesis, Shakespeare must have planned—as he introduced the discrepancies into Acts I and II—to rewrite the latter part of the play so as to bring it into agreement with the new ideas he was using. Then, when he came to do so, he decided that he could avoid the trouble—that he would not dull device by coldness and delay. Shakespeare must have been completely aware of the fact that the events and time sequences of the two parts of *Othello* were not in agreement, but he rightly guessed that on the stage this would not destroy the illusion of reality.

This way of accounting for the so-called double time in *Othello* explains as well the other contradictions in the two parts of the play mentioned above: Shakespeare's greater dependence on Cinthio in the second part, the change in atmosphere, the new account of Othello's wooing, the disappearance of Iago's motives, and the lack of any reference to the character of Cassio's fault in the latter part of the play. Most important, it explains the sudden change in the relations between Othello and Desdemona. For we cannot shut our eyes to the fact that at the end of Act II they are consummating their marriage and that from the beginning of Act III on they have been long married.

Some of the indications that Othello and Desdemona have suddenly ceased to be newlyweds at the beginning of Act III are still to be discussed. There is justice in Rymer's objection that Desdemona's great and energetic interest in Cassio's affairs on the morning after her first night of marriage seems out of place. And Cassio's application to her for help in regaining his post seems equally out of place—early in the morning after her wedding night. Desdemona speaks with more assurance of her ability to sway her husband than one would expect of a bride, and the same is true of her attitude of camaraderie toward Cassio—it is not that of a woman who has just been married. And nowhere in the latter part of the play do Desdemona and Othello speak like a newly married couple. Othello tells her:

I shall not dine at home   (III, iii, 58)

and makes to her the request a few lines later:

Leave me but a little to myself   (III, iii, 85)

both in a manner much different from his romantic attitude towards her in Acts I and II; and we have already noted how on the night of the same day she asks that her wedding sheets be laid

82

on the bed—as if they were remembrances of the past. This all adds to the feeling we have from the beginning of Act III that Shakespeare is not representing the house of a couple who have just consummated their marriage.[19]

The problem of Roderigo remains. He does not enter the last three acts until he is brought in (in IV, ii and V, i) to help Iago try to murder Cassio. And there is evidence that Shakespeare had not developed the Roderigo of Acts I and II when he wrote these two scenes.

Note the generality of Roderigo's recriminations against Iago in IV, ii. He says nothing about having sold his land, about having followed Iago to Cyprus, or about Cassio's having tried to beat him into a twiggen bottle. He merely says:

I do not find that thou deal'st justly with me...Every day thou daff'st me with some device, Iago, and rather, as it seems to me now, keep'st from me all conveniency than suppliest me with the least advantage of hope...I have wasted myself out of means. (IV, ii, 174–88)

The generality of this complaint makes it seem probable that when Shakespeare wrote it he had not yet written the scenes in Acts I and II in which Roderigo appears.[20] Note, too, Roderigo's statement:

You have...returned me expectations and comforts of sudden respect and acquaintance.
(IV, ii, 190–3)

and his threat a few lines later:

I will make myself known to Desdemona. (199–200)

These words are altogether out of keeping with Act I, scene I, in which it is made clear that Roderigo is a rejected suitor of Desdemona's. There Brabantio recognizes him and tells him:

In honest plainness thou hast heard me say
My daughter is not for thee. (I, i, 97–8)

Moreover, Roderigo here in Act IV first dwells on the *jewels* he has bought for Desdemona. He says:

The jewels you have had from me to deliver to Desdemona would half have corrupted a votarist.
(IV, iii, 188–90)

and later:

If she will return me my jewels, I will give over my suit and repent my unlawful solicitation.
(200–2)

Jewels are not mentioned in any of the conversations with Iago in Acts I and II. And Iago here makes no reference to what he has claimed at their earlier meetings—that Cassio is an impediment to Roderigo's hopes of enjoying Desdemona. This would have been an excellent argument by which to persuade Roderigo to kill Cassio, and the fact that Iago does not even mention it is perhaps the most striking indication that when Shakespeare wrote this scene he had not yet written the earlier scenes in which Roderigo appears. If Shakespeare had done this scene after them—in the ordinary order of composition—he might very well have adduced the new argument that Cassio must be killed to prevent Othello from taking Desdemona into Mauritania, but it seems unlikely that he would have failed to mention the other arguments, too. And his failure to do so is particularly significant at the end of this scene, when, obviously feeling that he has not convinced Roderigo that he must murder Cassio, he says merely:

I will show you such a necessity in his death that you shall think yourself bound to put it on him.

(IV, ii, 246–8)

Does it seem probable that Shakespeare would have been content with giving Iago this lame and impotent conclusion if he had already written the scenes in which Iago informs Roderigo that Desdemona is in love with Cassio? Also, when Roderigo and Iago are waiting to attack Cassio in v, i they again fail to make any reference to Iago's earlier arguments against Cassio. We would expect Iago to say something about how Cassio deserves death because he has taken Desdemona from Roderigo. Instead, he says merely:

It makes us or it mars us—think on that. (v, i, 4)

And Roderigo soliloquizes:

I have no great devotion to the deed,
And yet he hath given me satisfying reasons.
'Tis but a man gone. Forth my sword—he dies! (v, i, 8–10)

It must be observed, of course, that in the final scene of the play Cassio does refer to a letter found on Roderigo's body, and says that in it Roderigo

...upbraids Iago that he made him
Brave me upon the watch. (v, ii, 325–6).

If our thesis is to be accepted, this is to be explained as an attempt by Shakespeare to reconcile in some slight measure the two parts of the play. As Brents Stirling has pointed out in his essay on revisions in *Julius Caesar*, insertions naturally lead to such additions.[21] The most surprising feature of the two parts of *Othello* is the fact that Shakespeare did not make greater efforts to reconcile them in this last scene—that this is the only example of such an effort.

IV

It seems proper now to examine any possible evidence that the above explanation of the double time in *Othello* is wrong. Are all the contradictions in time the result of the hasty joining of the two disparate parts? Does any of the double time remain when we consider Acts I and II on the one hand and Acts III, IV, and V on the other, separately? Is there any 'long time' in the first part of the play or 'short time' in the second?

Let us consider Acts I and II first. One evidence of supposed long time has been pointed out in them.

Iago says to Roderigo:

Our General's wife is now the general. (II, iii, 343–4)

Furness's claim that this indicates a passage of time since the opening of the play has been accepted by some of the double-time enthusiasts, but without sufficient reason. Changes in lovers take place very quickly in real life as well as in many of Shakespeare's plays. No one considers Romeo's transformation when he falls in love with Juliet or Leontes' suspicion of Hermione indications of long or double time. And remember that Iago has something to gain by exaggeration.

Turning to Acts III, IV and V, we find that there are no suggestions of short time—no indications that Desdemona and Othello have just arrived from Venice and have just consummated their marriage beyond the fact that Act III follows Act II and that no interval is indicated. But two lines in this part of the play have been taken to indicate that during the one day on which the last three acts take place a long time passed. Consider the following:

1. When Bianca scolds Cassio for having been a week away, Cassio replies:

> I have this while with leaden thoughts been pressed.   (III, iv, 177)

J. Dover Wilson believes that Cassio is here saying that he has been worried about his demotion for a week.[22] If so, this indicates that a week has passed since the opening of Act III. But Cassio says nothing about his demotion, and his claim that he has been unhappy while away from Bianca is a conventional reply to her complaint about the 'tedious' hours she has spent. Cassio is merely assuring her that he has not been making merry with other women. The week he has spent away from Bianca is therefore like the long time which is referred to throughout the latter part of the play. When Shakespeare wrote this part of *Othello* he seems to have been thinking of the time as having passed before Cassio's demotion.

2. Desdemona greets Cassio and Cassio replies:

> *Desdemona:* How now, good Cassio, what's the news with you?
> *Cassio:* Madam, my former suit.   (III, IV, 129–30)

On the face of it, this does make it appear that a long time has passed since Cassio first approached Desdemona in III, i. But no specific reference is made to time, and we are to consider that so much has happened since Desdemona and Cassio last saw each other that their words are not surprising. It is as if two soldiers who part before a battle should meet again after hours of fighting. Such a question and answer as Desdemona and Cassio exchange would then be natural.

By now the reasons for believing that *Othello* is not all of one piece—that the two parts cannot have been produced by Shakespeare in the usual manner—have been made clear. But the statement that Shakespeare apparently started with Acts III, IV, and V, and then turned to Acts I and II has perhaps not been sufficiently defended. Is it not possible, it might be asked, that he produced two complete versions of the play and then decided to use the first part of one version and the second part of the other? Or is it not possible that he wrote the first part of the play first and then shifted his point of view before writing the second part—intending as he did so to revise the first part, but finally deciding that it was unnecessary?

The reasons for believing that Shakespeare started with Act III are as follows:

Shakespeare reveals in the latter part of *Othello* that he has not yet made up his mind about the details of Acts I and II. The contradictions between the two parts of the play, such as the two versions of Othello's wooing and the two time sequences, might be explained by one of the other hypotheses, but Shakespeare's complete *silence* about so many of the events of Acts I and II can only be explained by the supposition that he had not yet written them. And this explanation is supported by the fact that beginning with Act III when Cassio makes his first suit to

Desdemona the play is much closer to Cinthio than in the first two acts. It seems probable that Shakespeare remembered Cinthio better when he started to write than when he came to fill in with Acts I and II. It is significant that the events in the first part of the drama which were listed above as being 'forgotten' in the latter part were all added by Shakespeare to what he found in Cinthio.

Though it seems clear that Shakespeare did not plan the double time in *Othello* and that it is therefore not a proof of his skill in plot construction, the success of the play adds all the more lustre to Shakespeare's greatness, for it shows us how his other virtues as a dramatist can make audiences oblivious to such flaws. Iago, Othello, Desdemona, Emilia, and Cassio are so lifelike, so convincing that when we suffer with them—in the study as well as in the theatre—we pay no attention to such minor inconsistencies as that of the time sequences. In fact, the character portrayal in *Othello* is so satisfactory that many critics—some of whom have thought the double-time scheme a flaw—have praised its structure beyond that of all Shakespeare's other plays.[23]

But the evidences of imperfection remain. That Shakespeare wrote the last three acts of *Othello* about a Moor and a Venetian lady who had been married for some time would certainly be assumed by anyone who read only these three acts. And such a person would be quite unable to give an account of what happened to them before they arrived in Cyprus. He would know that Desdemona deceived her father when she married Othello—that, as Iago says, she seeled her father's eyes up close as oak—and that she refused other matches before she married Othello. So much of the latter part of the play is well linked with the first part.[24] But he would have a false idea about how the wooing took place. Moreover, he would know nothing about the attack on Cyprus by the Turks or about Cassio's drunkenness. He would be unable to guess that Iago has made earlier use of Roderigo in his plot against Cassio or even that he has told Roderigo the same lie he has told Othello—that Cassio is Desdemona's lover. As we have noted, at their last meeting the only argument by which Iago persuades Roderigo to kill Cassio is that his death will prevent Othello from taking Desdemona into Mauritania. What the other 'satisfying reasons' are we are not told. Why? Because Shakespeare had not yet decided what they would be. And after he *had* decided—while writing Acts I and II—he preferred not to tamper with Acts III, IV and V.

These contradictions in *Othello* are the source of many of the questions which have arisen in the minds of critics. The tragedy has come to be considered almost as much a problem play as *Measure for Measure* or *All's Well that Ends Well*. Coleridge explained away some of the lack of unity between the two parts of the tragedy by calling Iago's soliloquies the 'motive hunting of motiveless malignity'. E. E. Stoll's 'convention of the calumniator believed' was an attempt to explain why the unsuspicious Moor of Acts I and II becomes so jealous in Act III. L. L. Schücking tried to show that the contradictions in *Othello* are no different from those in other plays.

The problem of course, is why Shakespeare made a play by splicing together two parts not originally written to go together. The fact that *Othello* was not printed during Shakespeare's lifetime makes a theory that the contradictions are the result of post-Shakespearian alterations at first glance attractive. Can someone have revised *Othello* as Middleton or some other playwright almost certainly revised *Macbeth*? If such were the case, the two accounts of Othello's wooing could, like the two accounts of Macbeth's relations with the Thane of Cawdor, be blamed on an uninspired meddler. But there is no possibility of such a solution—nothing in

Othello like the un-Shakespearian speeches of Hecate—no dances, the addition of which could have made the excision of Shakespearian matter necessary. The problem is also unlike that in *Cymbeline*, in which Posthumus's dream is often thought to be below the Shakespearian level, or in *The Tempest* where the same has been said of the pageant presented by spirits to the young lovers. And *Othello* is again far different from *Timon of Athens*, part of which is so inferior that it is usually assumed to have been produced before or after Shakespeare created the torso of that play. Both parts of *Othello* seem equally Shakespearian.

Schücking's theories have been mentioned, and it may appear that all the contradictions between the two parts of *Othello* can be explained by the elucidation of Shakespeare's writing habits which Schücking gives us in his *Character Problems in Shakespeare's Plays*.[25] But Schücking has failed to observe that many problem passages in Shakespeare's plays cannot be explained as mere examples of what he calls 'Shakespeare's tendency to episodic intensification' (p. 119), as bits which Shakespeare put in—on the spur of the moment—for reasons of dramatic expediency. For many of the problem passages are more than bits. They are large blocks of material which cannot be conceived of as having been produced during the normal process of writing a play.

To put together in a drama materials not originally written as a unit was not extraordinary in Shakespeare's time. Someone made several additions to Kyd's *Spanish Tragedy*, for instance, and there are the speeches by Hecate in *Macbeth*. Shakespeare represents Hamlet as making an insertion in *The Murder of Gonzago*. Most important, there is textual evidence of insertions by Shakespeare himself in his own plays. The most striking examples are Theseus' speech about the lunatic, the lover, and the poet, in v, i of *A Midsummer-Night's Dream* and Mercutio's Queen-Mab speech in I, iv of *Romeo and Juliet*, both of which indicate by the mislining of their verse in the quarto editions that they were apparently inserted in the margins of the manuscripts. Moreover, Brents Stirling has argued convincingly that in *Julius Caesar* the meeting of the conspirators (I, i) and the twice-rendered disclosure of Portia's death (IV, iii) both contain evidence of revision.[26] The contradictions between these passages and the plays in which they appear are obviously not to be explained by Schücking's theory of episodic intensification, and the same is true of the contradictions between the two parts of *Othello*. It is possible to account for them only by supposing that these parts were not originally written to go together—without, at least, extensive changes which were never made.

It may be hard to picture a playwright of Shakespeare's ability as having joined two parts of *Othello* not originally intended to go together, or as having combined imperfectly unified material in the plays mentioned above. At any rate, however, the hypothesis that Shakespeare put together in *Othello* parts not originally written as a unit appears more acceptable than the hypothesis that the play was born whole but imperfectly formed in his mind. The former procedure would have at least the advantage of economy. The latter can have no satisfactory explanation.

V

Though Shakespeare may often have made insertions in his plays, *Othello* appears to be the only one in which the inharmonious material is of such magnitude that the drama may be said to fall into two parts. Except for passages short enough to be called insertions, the other plays are well knit, and their beginnings and endings—compared with *Othello*, at least—are well linked together.

We find no such links between the two parts of *Othello* as we do, for instance, between parts of *Hamlet*. The relation between such passages in that play as III, ii, 297–301; III, iii, 80–4; IV, iv, 1–4; V, i, 154–64; and V, ii, 64–8, shows clearly that when Shakespeare was writing the latter part of *Hamlet* he remembered not merely the general outline of the earlier part of the story but the details of what he had written. Except for Iago's statement that Desdemona's father had suspected Othello of witchcraft, we have no such reminiscences in *Othello*—rather a whole series of equally striking contradictions.

Note also the links between the latter part of *Macbeth* and the beginning:

1   Thou hast it now—King, Cawdor, Glamis, all,
    As the Weird Women promis'd; and I fear
    Thou play'dst most foully for't. Yet it was said
    It should not stand in thy posterity,
    But that myself should be the root and father
    Of many kings.   (III, i, 1–6)

2   He chid the sisters
    When first they put the name of king upon me,
    And bade them speak to him. Then, prophetlike,
    They hail'd him father to a line of kings.   (III, i, 57–60)

3   O proper stuff!
    This is the very painting of your fear.
    This is the air-drawn dagger which you said
    Led you to Duncan.   (III, iv, 60–3)

4   Out, damned spot! out, I say! One, two. Why then 'tis time to do't. Hell is murky. Fie, my lord, fie! A soldier and afeard? What need we fear who knows it, when none can call our pow'r to accompt? Yet who would have thought the old man to have had so much blood in him?   (V, i, 39–45)

Even the separate history plays are better integrated with one another than are the two parts of *Othello*. If Shakespeare had shown the same lack of interest in linking *Richard II* to *Henry IV* that he showed when he placed Act II and Act III of *Othello* side by side, he would never have had Bolingbroke ask in the earlier play, 'Can no one tell me of my unthrifty son?' Nor would he have taken the trouble to represent Hotspur as a mere boy when he met Bolingbroke at Berkeley Castle.[27] We can be sure, at any rate, that if Shakespeare *had* made Hotspur in *Richard II* as old as Bolingbroke, critics would explain the contradiction with *Henry IV* by the fact that the two plays were written at different times and in different frames of mind.

NOTES

1. Scholars and critics have not always paid careful attention to Cinthio. Cf. Ned B. Allen, 'Who Stole the Handkerchief?', *Notes and Queries*, n.s., II (1955), 292.

2. The critics are mistaken who claim that Cinthio's stories are not fitted to their narrators. Cinthio fails, of course, to accommodate his tales to those who tell them as well as does Chaucer, but he usually observes dramatic propriety in allotting them. A kind of battle of the sexes is indicated by the fact that the men (with the exception of Curtio) usually tell stories about debauched women, while the women tell about equally debauched men. Moreover, the individual men and women can often be distinguished by the tales they tell. Curtio is certainly the most proper narrator of either sex.

3. Cinthio's villain does, however, get a devilish satisfaction out of the Moor's suffering.

4. In Cinthio, the maid of the *Capo di squadra* has it.

5. In Cinthio, this request is made only to the Alfiero's wife.

6. In his preface to *Othello*, J. Dover Wilson observes that *Othello* is the 'tensest and swiftest of the tragedies' (New Cambridge ed. 1957, p. xxxi). But this is not true of Acts I and II. They are less tense and swift than the first two acts of most of the other tragedies—*Hamlet*, *King Lear*, and *Macbeth*, for instance.

7. One wonders why this assistance was necessary from Cassio or from anyone else, since, according to Othello's story in Act I, the wooing was over as soon as he realized that it had begun.

8. Thomas Rymer, *A Short View of Tragedy*, reprinted in *The Works of Thomas Rymer*, ed. Curt A. Zimansky (New Haven, 1956), pp. 150 ff.; P. A. Daniel, 'Time Analyses of the Plots of Shakespeare's Plays', *Transactions of the New Shakespeare Society* (1877–9), pp. 224–32; F. G. Fleay, Robinson's *Epitome of Literature*, 15 June 1879; Mabel Buland, 'The Presentation of Time in the Elizabethan Drama', *Yale Studies in English*, XLIV (New Haven, 1912).

9. John Wilson's articles first appeared in *Blackwood's Magazine*, November 1849, April 1850, and May 1850. They were reprinted in substance in *Transactions of the New Shakespeare Society*, 1875–76 and 1877–79, and in the Furness *Variorum* ed. of *Othello*, pp. 358–72.

10. Cf. Harley Granville-Barker, *Prefaces to Shakespeare* (1947), II, 24–30; J. Dover Wilson, *op. cit.* pp. xxx–xxxvi; M. R. Ridley, ed., The New Arden *Othello* (1958), p. lxx; and also Peter Alexander, *Shakespeare's Life and Art* (1939), p. 166.

11. *Art and Artifice in Shakespeare* (Cambridge, 1933), pp. 26–7.

12. A. C. Bradley observes in *Shakespearean Tragedy* (1904) that the two time schemes exist in the two parts of the play (pp. 423–9), but he has no solution for the problem, and he does not connect it with the other contradictions in the two parts of the drama.

13. A similar sudden time speed-up occurs at one point in Act III. The opening of III, iii is presumably early in the morning, since Cassio has arranged for the meeting in the same scene in which he hired the musicians to bid Othello 'good morrow'. But a few lines later Desdemona says:

> Your dinner and the generous islanders
> By you invited do attend your presence.
>
> (280–1)

Like the speedy disembarkments of Act II, however, this quick passage of time does not conflict with any other time scheme.

14. Only a short examination of the facts is necessary to make it clear how little justification there is for Granville-Barker's claim that time in *Othello* is 'contracted and expanded like a concertina' (p. 10).

15. Othello does say in III, iv, 53 that an Egyptian gave the handkerchief to his mother, and in V, ii, 216 that his father gave it to her. But such minor discrepancies are to be found in all the plays.

16. Scene ii of Act III, with its reference to Othello's duties to the state and to the fortification he is about to inspect, seems to have been written to let the audience know that Othello is in charge of Cyprus. If Shakespeare had just written Acts I and II, it is unlikely that he would have considered the scene necessary. One wonders why he did not finally omit it, but his failure to do so is explained by the fact that the scene has another function: it provides time for Cassio to make his petition to Desdemona off stage. If Shakespeare had deleted it, he would have had to produce another short scene to take its place—or let us see Cassio's meeting with Desdemona—and the many contradictions which he allowed to remain in the two parts of the play make it clear that he was in no mood for such revisions.

17. It seems unlikely, too, that Shakespeare would have failed to have Iago refer to Cassio's drunkenness in the temptation scene if he had written II, iii before it. Absence of any such reference is particularly striking in III, iii, 246 ff., where Iago says:

> Though it be fit that Cassio have his place...

18. Some rationalists unwilling to accept the miracle of double time have been driven to other shifts. They have explained Iago's claim that Cassio said in his sleep:

Cursed fate that gave thee to the Moor (III, iii, 426)

by postulating a contract marriage between Othello and Desdemona, which they suppose took place before the marriage we hear about in the opening scene of the play, shutting their eyes to such lines as Othello's:

That profit's yet to come 'tween me and you
(II, iii, 10)

and Iago's:

He hath not yet made wanton the night with her and she is sport for Jove. (II, iii, 16–17)

And they explain the references to Cassio's long acquaintance with Bianca by arguing that Cassio must have brought her with him (or have been followed by her) when he came to Cyprus from Venice. Some scholars have even tried to prove that it was a usual practice in Shakespeare's time for soldiers to take their prostitutes with them on foreign expeditions. These critics cite Cassio's words:

I was the other day talking on the seabank with certain Venetians; and thither comes the bauble, and, by this hand, she falls me thus about my neck...
(IV, i, 136–9)

The mention of Venetians proves, they say, that this is supposed to have happened in Venice. This is, of course illogical. In fact, it indicates just the opposite. For if Shakespeare had been thinking of Cassio as relating what had happened in Venice, he would not have him say that he was talking with Venetians—that would have been taken for granted. His mentioning the fact that they were Venetians, then, makes it clear that this is assumed to have taken place in Cyprus.

19. It is perhaps significant that all seven instances of the use of the name *Desdemon* instead of *Desdemona* occur in the last three acts of the Folio version of the play. (*Desdemona* is used throughout the Quarto). Though this by no means proves that Shakespeare wrote the two parts of the play separately, in two frames of mind, it lends support to that belief. Perhaps Shakespeare started in the last three acts to call her *Desdemon* as well as *Desdemona*. But when he began to work on the exposition, he went over to the form *Desdemona*, for that form alone is used in Acts I and II. In the last three acts, nearly all the examples of the form *Desdemona* occur in prose passages or at the ends of lines of blank verse. Perhaps Shakespeare used *Desdemon* throughout Acts III, IV, and V, and then he (or someone else) changed it to *Desdemona* when this could be done without destroying the metre. In view of the likelihood

of minor changes in the manuscript by copyists or compositors after it left Shakespeare's hands, however, this is not so significant as the other contradictions between the two parts of the play. We can merely observe that the *Desdemon* form *may* be authorial and that if so it has some significance when added to the other indications that the play was not written as a unit.

20. The absence here of links with their earlier meetings is very different from what we find in Act II, scenes i and iii. In the first, Iago says:

I have brought you from Venice, (II, i, 270)

and in the second Roderigo says:

I have been tonight exceedingly well cudgell'd; and I think the issue will be—I shall have so much experience for my pains; and so, with no money at all, and a little more wit, return again to Venice.
(II, iii, 370–5)

21. '*Julius Caesar* in Revision', *Shakespeare Quarterly*, XIII (1962), pp. 187–205. See especially pp. 202–3.

22. *Op. cit.* p. xxxv.

23. Cf. R. G. Moulton, *Shakespeare as Dramatic Artist* (Oxford, 1897), chapter XI; Bradley, p. 177; Sir Walter Raleigh, *Shakespeare* (1907), p. 142; John W. Draper, *The 'Othello' of Shakespeare's Audience* (Paris, 1952), p. 202; J. Dover Wilson, pp. xxxv–xxxvi; and F. R. Leavis, *The Common Pursuit* (1962), p. 136. Leavis ends his commendation of *Othello* as a creation which is unblurred and undistracted by cloudy recessions with the statement: 'There would, it seems, be something like a consensus in this sense.'

Even in the eighteenth century the structure of *Othello* was highly praised. Samuel Johnson's comment is especially interesting. In his introduction to *Othello*, he observes: 'Had the scene opened in Cyprus and the preceding incidents been occasionally related, there had been little wanting to a drama of the most exact and scrupulous regularity.'

24. One of the references to Desdemona's father in Act IV is not altogether in harmony with what we learn of him in Act I. When Lodovico brings news that Othello has been recalled to Venice, Desdemona says:

If haply you my father do suspect
An instrument of this your calling back,
Lay not your blame on me; if you have lost him
Why I have lost him too. (IV, ii, 44–7)

This is not, of course, so strikingly at variance with what has happened before the Senate in Venice as are other things in the latter part of the play, but, in view of the other contradictions between the two parts, it seems likely that Desdemona is here indicating that the recall of Othello has given him such reason to suspect that he has 'lost' her father that she finds it necessary to make it clear that she is ranging herself with Othello, not with Brabantio. If this is what Shakespeare intended her to imply, it is, of course, out of keeping with I, iii. In that scene Brabantio leaves no room for doubt that both Desdemona and Othello have lost him. Moreover, if Shakespeare had already written I, iii when he wrote the end of the play, does it seem likely that he would have failed to have Lodovico announce Brabantio's death to Desdemona as soon as he arrived from Venice? As it is, we are told about his death only at the end—and by Gratiano, who seems to have been introduced for this sole purpose. This sounds like a late insertion. It is perhaps significant, too, that Desdemona's father is not called Brabantio in the last three acts.

25. New York, 1922.

26. Stirling, *op. cit.* pp. 192–205.

27. Another similar link is the statement of the Chief Justice to Falstaff in *Henry IV:*

Your day's service at Shrewsbury hath a little gilded over your night's exploit on Gadshill.

(I, ii, 168–70)

OTHELLO: A TRAGEDY BUILT ON A COMIC STRUCTURE

BY

BARBARA HELIODORA C. DE MENDONÇA

In Professor H. B. Charlton's *Shakespearian Tragedy* there is an extremely satisfactory interpretation of *Othello*[1] in which two main points should be noted: the tragedy issues from the marriage between two people of widely different backgrounds, and Othello is to be accepted, not as the victim of Iago but as a fully developed tragic hero who is entirely responsible for the tragedy and its consequences. My own views about the main interpretation of *Othello* are so similar to those of Charlton that I assume that any staging of the tragedy must, ultimately, create the picture which he achieves through critical analysis. That picture was originally created by Shakespeare through dramatic and theatrical means, and this article is aimed at the clarification of a very specific aspect of the theatrical language which the author used in a work of art which only attains its full significance when it is presented on a stage.

Even though he never cheapens his work in order to be understood I am convinced that Shakespeare, used as he was to writing for a widely varied audience, at all times wished to make the main structure of his plays, their plots and characters, as clear as possible. This does not mean that his plays will not have many layers of deeper significance, or that to be fully understood they will not depend on the capacity of each individual to react imaginatively to all that is offered by dialogue, characterization, plot and poetry; but it does mean that in *Othello*, as elsewhere, Shakespeare reached out to his public through visual and eminently stageworthy elements which time and fashion have made us forget or overlook.

In writing the tragedy of *Othello* Shakespeare used with supreme mastery an unexpected but immensely effective theatrical idiom, which could only be used by someone with great insight into human nature and great mastery of dramatic and theatrical technique. If *Othello* was to deal with the marriage between 'an erring barbarian and a super-subtle Venetian', Shakespeare's prime consideration would be—granted that it was written for stage and audience—that the idea of this contrast should become clear and easily recognizable to the public. The first act, which takes place in Venice, must then be considered in its full significance, i.e. as an instrument of the definition of the world to which Desdemona belonged and to which very significantly Othello did not.

How was the average Elizabethan, in those days of difficult travel, to identify Venice? Shakespeare chose the simplest and most obvious means available to someone who lived in the world of the theatre and was writing for regular theatre-goers: the *commedia dell'arte*, a highly theatrical instrument, which was not only Italian but also largely Venetian. That both Shakespeare and the Elizabethans were conversant with *commedia dell'arte* is easy to prove from the records transcribed in, for instance, Sir Edmund Chambers's *The Elizabethan Stage*, and for this specific play the form had the advantage of not only identifying the Venetian environment but also of criticizing it, a technique which is the basis of all the best forms of comedy. If the erring barbarian was to be shown as morally more demanding than the super-subtle Venetians, the critical attitude towards Venetian society was indispensable. The placing of the action of *Othello* against this Venetian *commedia dell'arte* background has, to me, opened such stageworthy possibilities for a correct picture of the issues at stake that I have become convinced that one must accept the rather strange fact that it is a tragedy built on a comic structure. From this fact, for instance, would easily spring the explanation for the widely spread notion of the exceptional cruelty of *Othello*: it is exceptionally cruel because, from the initial dramatic situation, one does not expect tragedy but comedy, and it is only Shakespeare's mastery that makes it possible for tragedy to emerge from Cinthio's plot without any breach of tone and without evading the issue. The secret, of course, lies in the presence, in that structure, of the non-Venetian element, Othello himself.

The influence of *commedia dell'arte* on *Othello* can be felt in different ways, and structure, characterization and conflict must be examined separately. To begin with structure it must be remembered, first of all, that of all the tragedies *Othello* is the only one that relies largely on plot for its development, which is in itself a characteristic of comedy rather than of tragedy. And in this comic structure of plot is to be considered Iago's position as *meneur-de-jeu*, as Zanni, as Harlequin, above all as Brighella; no matter what the name, he is a servant who is working for his own advancement when he should be serving his master. The very idea of advancement, which is so important in Shakespeare, does not exist at all in Cinthio, and yet it is one of the most important aspects of Zanni.

The structure of the opening scene of *Othello* can lead to rather surprising conclusions, when taken by itself, and when all knowledge of the nature of the play as a whole is omitted. The scene, from the action, can be identified as taking place in a street in Venice, in front of a house with a window above and a door below. That particular scenic disposition is described by Emilio Del Carro in his *Nel Regno Delle Maschere* as typical of *commedia dell'arte* where the windows and doors made the fixed setting more flexible.[2] As the action opens two men are talking and one of them, Iago, is obviously indignant because he had not been promoted to lieutenant (a *lèse-majesté* crime in terms of any Zanni's ego), claiming further that 'three great ones of the city' had 'off capped' to the general on his behalf. This is an obvious lie, because if these men had really existed Iago would know their names and quote them whenever possible. We also learn that the general, who is described in most disparaging terms, has married the daughter of the old man in front of whose house they are standing, and that Iago plans to arouse the old father to tell him of the elopement. But when Brabantio does appear at his window Iago takes care to stay hidden and unidentified, pushing forward the foolish Roderigo to be the overt bearer of the news. Roderigo, lacking both wit and courage, has to be prodded, which is no problem for Iago, who, it must be noted, not only makes jokes ('Thou art a villain' / 'You are a senator') but also uses the obscene language with which Arlecchino or Brighella always told Pantalone that he has lost his daughter.

There are further episodes in the structure that are closer to the world of comedy than to that of tragedy: the loss of an article (such as Desdemona's handkerchief) and its subsequent use by someone in a position to give the loss a compromising significance is one such, but the most classically comic situation of the play is the conversation between Iago and Cassio about Bianca played in such a way that Othello should think that they are talking about Desdemona. Such misguided notions, such tricks, can hardly be classified among well established tragic situations.

Without considering Iago's intentions, and considering exclusively the outward aspects of his actions, Richard Flatter in *The Moor of Venice* compares Iago with a *commedia dell'arte* character in that he decides on one line of action towards a person and then acts—or improvises—accordingly.[3] This inventiveness of Iago's, this seemingly inexhaustible ability to keep telling a different story to each different person, as well as the zest and virtuosity with which he keeps all the other characters from checking their stories, is perhaps of Iago's facets the most clearly borrowed from the typical Zanni. In his *Shakespeare and the Allegory of Evil* Bernard Spivack claims, justifiably, that Iago is a direct descendant of the Vice of medieval moralities,[4] but to that very valid idea I should like to add the suggestion that in theatrical terms Shakespeare borrowed from that other and nearer forefather, the Zanni-Arlecchino-Brighella of the *commedia dell'arte*, where Vice had already become less allegorical, more flexible, more adapted to the individualized drama of the Elizabethan times.

Of all incarnations of Zanni Iago seems to be most closely linked with the morose and cruel Brighella. In Thelma Niklaus's *Harlequin Phoenix*, for instance, we find the following description of Brighella: '...his mask, of a dingy yellowish-green, gave him the cynical expression of a man for whom life holds no more surprises...His brazen assurance carried him victoriously through his career of confidence trickster and hired bully. He was the interloper, the braggart, the eavesdropper, stealthy and sinister in his comings and goings, boding no good for anyone who came in contact with him, and always ready to sell his honour, his master...He took a savage delight in scoring off a friend or an enemy, in making trouble, in committing crimes. While Arlecchino was always amazed at the consequences of his own blunders, Brighella's villany was conscious and purposeful.'[5] It would be hard to take exception to such a description of Iago himself.

In the book just quoted the first two themes listed as characteristic of Italian comedy in its earliest Renaissance form are the deception of a master and the cuckolding of a husband, which brings us to yet another interesting link between *Othello* and comedy: from time immemorial the cuckold has been, for some mysterious reason, a source of unquenchable laughter, and the rather surprising conclusion that we come to on examining Iago's purposes in creating his whole intrigue is that his only intention was to make Othello ridiculous. How does that fit into a tragic pattern? Compare the intentions of other characters in other tragedies in regard to their opponents: Claudius plans exile and death for Hamlet, Hamlet plans death for Claudius; Macbeth, Brutus, Antony, Tybalt, Titus, all think of extreme, irreversible actions against those they know they must fight to survive; but Iago alone, of all major characters in the tragedies, comes up with the rather extraordinary idea that to take full revenge against the general who did not make him his lieutenant he will make that same general believe that his wife was unfaithful. Of course it is revenge, but revenge on a petty, comic level, because Iago's fertile but shallow imagination does not carry him beyond the simple desire to demoralize Othello. In the super-subtle Venetian world Othello would then become the laughing stock of society and—Iago would see to it—the army. But Zanni did not count on the unknown element, the reactions of the 'erring barbarian' to his petty provocation. Out of this disproportion Shakespeare creates tragedy.

Shakespeare's use of characters from the *commedia dell'arte* in his dramatis personae must also be considered. It would be useless to expect all such characters to put in an appearance or that those who are used should include all of the many possible facets of each; but nevertheless it will be shown that some *commedia dell'arte* characters do appear in *Othello* and that they can be easily identified.

Iago, inevitably, is the first to come to mind, because of the role as *meneur-de-jeu* from which, of course, stems the widespread notion that he is the most important element in the tragedy. But besides being responsible for the mechanical development of the intrigue Iago has many other aspects to connect him with Zanni-Brighella. First and foremost comes the theme of advancement, which does not appear in Giraldi Cinthio, but which is fundamental in Shakespeare and one of the most characteristic traits of the Italian comedy servants. In his Zanni and Harlequin incarnations the servant's very clothes, with their diamond design, are a development of the rags and patches of his beggarly origins, and his most typical activity is the plotting to gain something, be it promotion, be it food, be it money, regardless of the fact that, like his forefather Vice, he almost invariably ends up by getting a good beating instead of advancement. But what is surprising and really similar to Zanni-Arlecchino-Brighella is that at no point until the very end of the tragedy does Iago seem intent on the tragic downfall or death of Othello; his object is the demoralization of his master and his own advancement, to be gained as thanks for having played the sorry role of informer and 'protector' of Othello's honour. Even as late as the end of v, i, Iago still says 'This is the night/That either makes me or foredoes me quite', from which it must be gathered that even though he has gone as far as murder Iago still hopes to gain, by his wits, a satisfactory solution to the problem of his promotion. Such blindness concerning the far-reaching consequences of his own actions is typical of Zanni and, ultimately, of Brighella. Add to all this the vulgarity (not to say the obscenity) of Iago, his acute pleasure in finding or imagining rottenness in all purity or goodness (simply because these are alien to his own nature) and the picture of the Italian servant of the *commedia dell'arte* is complete.

But as a last touch of extraordinary similarity between Iago and Zanni there is the strange fact that the man who is described in the dramatis personae simply as 'a villain' should be known as 'honest Iago'. In the *commedia dell'arte*, also, many an intrigue hinges on the fact that a wily servant is considered trustworthy and consequently given all sorts of important tasks to perform. Both Iago and Zanni—like all successful confidence tricksters—depend for the success of their intrigues on the same misguided motion that they are 'honest'; and because of this acquired reputation they are in a privileged position to know both their masters' hopes and their weak spots. If Othello can be led by the nose, like an ass, so can many other characters in the play; if others refuse to believe Iago's accusations about Desdemona, it is because that is not their particular weak spot, and they are led to believe other stories. If Othello is so often criticized for believing Iago, it is because there is a sort of natural reaction resulting from our knowledge that tragedy will come from his believing it, but to criticize Othello and not Cassio, and not Desdemona, and not Roderigo, and not Emilia for precisely the same thing, i.e., believing the tale carefully calculated to be accepted by that particular individual, is to criticize emotionally, under the influence of *a posteriori* knowledge; in his true world of comedy Zanni is always believed for the same reasons that Iago is believed: he tells credible stories to the people most likely to believe them.

Another classic *commedia dell'arte* mask which appears almost intact in *Othello* is Pantalone. About the Brabantio-Pantalone relationship Miss K. M. Lea wrote: 'The description of Brabantio as a "magnifico" in *Othello* is appropriate without any thought of Italian comedy, but his position as a frantic father is so like that of Pantalone that we can hardly avoid the double allusion.'[6] Brabantio is, in fact, a surprisingly conventional presentation of the role of the old fool whose daughter marries against his wishes. Being called out of bed in the middle of the night and made fun of by disreputable characters standing beneath his window who tell him to examine his household to see if nothing has been stolen is indeed the lot of Pantalone in his father role. Furthermore, considering that Shakespeare used elements of comic structure to criticize Venetian society, it is worthwhile to reflect on the moral temper of a father who, to take revenge on Othello, is willing to allow with no great misgivings that his own daughter is capable of adultery: 'She has deceived her father, and may thee.' If Desdemona's own father could make such a prediction, is it surprising that Othello should believe Iago's accusations? But from Pantalone the sentence is to be expected.

Roderigo, who is not in Cinthio and first appears in the comic opening scene, is the dupe who gives money to the *meneur-de-jeu* to obtain the hand or the favours of the heroine, a rather well-known character in *commedia dell'arte* who appears later, for instance, in Molière's *L'Ecole des femmes*, a classic example of influence of Italian comedy. Thinking that his lady can be bought this sorry figure serves the double purpose of showing not only that he is himself a fool, and a corrupt fool at that, but also Zanni-Iago in one of his worst aspects, that of a pandar.

It is not difficult to identify Desdemona with the 'amorosa' or 'innamorata' of the professionals' comedy. She is sweet, charming, true to her love but, like all her sisters, motherless and fully determined to stand up against paternal authority in defence of her love. Certainly this is not all that there is to be said about Desdemona, but it is significant that while Shakespeare gave her many other characteristics and a much richer moral texture he preserved these fundamental traits. Cinthio, for instance, mentions that the marriage of Desdemona to the Moor was opposed by 'i parenti', i.e., parents or relatives, so that the definite lack of a mother becomes yet one more detail added by Shakespeare that fits into the *commedia dell'arte* scheme.

The professionals' comedy was not exclusively Venetian and the term must, in part, be accepted as meaning Italian or European, as opposed to the non-European Othello. So there is nothing in Cassio's citizenship as a Florentine to stop him from being identified as an 'innamorato'. On this identification Iago depends for the apparent plausibility of his accusations; Cassio has all the social graces and all the standard virtues (and vices) of the well-bred Italian of the Renaissance. It is possible, today, to take exception to Cassio's treatment of Bianca, but according to the mores of his time he is as conventional in his respect for Desdemona as he is in his disrespect for Bianca. Bianca herself cannot be considered as an individual but only as that standard inhabitant of the world of *commedia dell'arte*, the courtesan, whose dramatic function was always to make complicated intrigues yet more complicated.

Neither does Emilia fall outside the range of *commedia dell'arte* characters. In Allardyce Nicoll's *The World of Harlequin*, for instance, one may find the following references to the serving maid: 'Active though the servetta usually shows herself, she does not form one of the focal points of these comedies...in 1600 she was both older and rougher than in 1700...quite clear that she is intended to be a woman with ample experience of the ways of the world...Light-hearted and loyal to her mistress...takes a fair share in the intrigue but this share is peripheral rather than central.'[7] There is not much more that one may say about Emilia.

It would be pointless to look for further parallels in minor characters; they are not involved in the intrigue itself and Shakespeare was not writing *commedia dell'arte*, but only making use of some aspects of it to establish certain points of reference in his tragedy.

Even more pointless would be to include any possibility of an interpretation of Othello himself into this scheme (in spite of the fairly common presence of Moorish and eastern elements in many a *commedia dell'arte* plot) since the very essence of the conflict lies in the fact that he is not a super-subtle Venetian. After the *commedia dell'arte* opening scene the first appearance of Othello himself in scene ii, after all the disparaging remarks that have been made about him, still in a Venetian background, talking to an Iago who insists on talking in terms of petty intrigue, should be as impressive, as unexpected, as contrasting as the presence of Hamlet in suits of solemn black amidst the colourful court of Denmark. What is often called Othello's naïveté, in fact, is something very akin to the passion for moral absolutes that makes Hamlet react to certain facts in a manner far different from that of those who surround him. If he is accepted as such a man Othello can hardly be blamed for believing a man with an uncanny capacity for making up plausible stories and for spotting people's weak points, particularly when he is not the only character in the play who does not investigate the veracity of Iago's assertions. What Iago arouses is not only Othello's jealousy but his implacable sense of justice; and except for that saddest of all moments, the few seconds during which he wants to escape the responsibility for the murder of Desdemona, Othello does in fact act according to his very exacting sense of justice both towards Desdemona and towards himself.

The Venetian first act, then, serves most admirably the purpose of establishing both visually and psychologically the nature of the background of these two people who marry on the strength of an overwhelmingly romantic love; Desdemona's is shown in detail because the public must be able to see, as Othello was able to see, what was the world to which she belonged—socially if not morally; Othello's is created implicitly by the contrast between his own powerful personality and all that surrounds him. Once Venice has played its part we move on to Cyprus, to the neutrality of a military fortress; in this strange and distant place the protagonists of the tragedy are left without the protection of either of their two worlds, with Othello in full command, with the authority and responsibility to punish all those who break the law.

And so we come to the tragic situation. The means that Shakespeare uses to make a tragedy out of Cinthio's melodrama are in themselves rather subtle: at no point is Othello presented as gauche or in any way socially inadequate; on the contrary, seldom if ever has Shakespeare created a character as noble, as majestic, as respected, as well-loved as Othello. The fundamental conflict between the Moor and Venice does not arise from social behaviour but from moral convictions which are more impassioned and more exacting than those of the super-subtle Venetians who lived in a world of excessive civilization whose social usages permitted certain attitudes and gestures which had, from habit, become empty of significance, but which could—particularly in moments of emotional stress—be exploited by Iago as being the outward show of supposed moral flaws. One case in point would be the greetings between Desdemona and Cassio on arrival in Cyprus; to a Venetian such behaviour is perfectly natural, but Iago tries at once to give it a compromising interpretation.

Iago is himself a Venetian, but his continuous and all-exclusive preoccupation with himself and his own personal problems gives him the possibility of seeing the 'Venetians' of the play without any sort of emotional engagement. His own personal world and Othello's are so completely different that tragedy may evolve from the clashing of their different points of view. It has often been said, for instance, that Othello's reactions are disproportionately violent to Iago's provocations, but what does not seem to be said at all is that Shakespeare very specifically goes out of his way to show that a Venetian would not react to the issue of adultery in the same way as Othello. Iago, in fact, twice suggests that he suspects Emilia of infidelity with the general, and even though he does it in soliloquies (and consequently not to impress others) and claims that he will take violent action about it, he never does and seems, after a while, to forget the possibility altogether. To argue that Othello is a fool to react as he does to Iago on the subject of Desdemona is to leave out the main point about the whole tragedy which is that to Othello her adultery is to be considered from a moral attitude completely different from anyone else's in the play. Besides, her fellow-Venetians who do not believe even the possibility of Desdemona being unfaithful had known her for a long time, which Othello had not; and, most important of all, in Othello's case the accusation was not made about an acquaintance but about his own wife: her adultery would touch him directly, both in honour and in emotion, but not any of the others. Certainly Iago never believes the story himself, and most certainly he does not expect Othello to react as he does. The intrigue unleashes passions which Iago not only had never experienced personally but which he had never witnessed in any of the people who normally surrounded him. The world of absolutes, the world in which there can be no moral compromise, does not exist for Iago, just as without absolutes, with moral compromise, there can be no world for Othello. If he can be led by the nose like an ass, it is only because he could not conceive that anyone could behave in a manner different from what Christian doctrine had taught him to be right, because he could not conceive that it was possible for anyone not to have his own moral rectitude, dedication to justice and impartiality of judgement. Lacking malice, Othello is led to murder and suicide because it does not occur to him, not even in relation to Desdemona, whom he loves, that a statement of such grave nature made with apparent seriousness (and seemingly backed by at least circumstantial evidence) could be false.

The significance of the distance between these two worlds cannot be stressed too much, and in the staging of *Othello* the progressive shifting from the Venetian values of *commedia dell'arte* to Othello's extreme, rough and violent ones must be the key to the appalling emergence of a tragedy from what should be, from the initial given dramatic values, a comic situation. The tragedy that emerges is the kind that centuries later would be defined by Harold Pinter in the sentence 'The point about tragedy is that it is *no longer funny*',[8] and dead seriousness takes over because one man, Othello, cannot accept being made into a laughing stock as a cuckold.

Iago never comes to understand quite fully the issues at stake. His object was not tragedy, and his main purpose was never to prove that Desdemona was unfaithful. The real pity of the tragedy is that Iago's original motivation, promotion, and the intrigue about Desdemona and Cassio do not take on the significance that he expected them to. Iago is so anxious to start his sordid campaign, to take revenge for not having been appointed lieutenant, that he speaks too soon, i.e. before a period of time has elapsed to solidify the marriage and strengthen the bonds of mutual knowledge and trust between Othello and Desdemona, and touches too delicate a subject considering Othello's nature and background. His one authentic motive, advancement, then gets lost in the intrigue because for Othello the only thing that mattered was the moral issue of adultery. Only when this unexpected change in the motivation of the action is taken into consideration can it be seen that it is not entirely correct to believe that Iago really leads the sequence of events. His original notion leads him into unforeseen circumstances, and what he actually does, from the third act on, when through Othello's reaction he loses control of events, is to improvise constantly, as each new situation arises, in an attempt to bring the action back to his objective of becoming lieutenant. Like his prototype, the servant of Italian comedy, he is unable to think in any terms but those of his own interest.

Why indeed should Iago keep silent about his motives at the end of the tragedy if not because, like all Zannies, there was nothing for him to say. Here, more than at any other moment, he is kept near his origins: all Zannies, like Iago, have such petty motives for building their very intricate plots that to admit them in the end, particularly after having been found guilty, would be to reveal that they were nothing but blundering fools. In *Othello*, where the comic intrigue had reached tragic proportions, it would be even more impossible to admit that several lives had been lost—to say nothing of the tragic waste of the moral crisis of Othello—because a little man wanted a job that Othello, a very competent general, knew that he was not fit to hold.

If 1604 is accepted as the date for *Othello* one may not overlook the fact that as a man of the theatre Shakespeare must have watched with interest and curiosity the performances given in London in 1602 by 'Flaminio Curtesse' and his troupe of Italian players; with Cinthio's story in his hands and at the height of his dramatic and poetic powers, what was there to stop him from achieving the seemingly impossible task of using a comic structure to build a tragedy? Zanni, spinning his web of lies, not only gets caught in it himself but also sets in motion passions which he could neither feel emotionally nor understand intellectually. For once, in his long and varied career, Zanni blunders into the world of tragedy, but it took Shakespeare to see the full theatrical possibilities of such a blunder.

© BARBARA HELIODORA C. DE MENDONÇA 1968

NOTES

1. H. B. Charlton, *Shakespearian Tragedy* (Cambridge, 1952).

2. E. Del Carro, *Nel Regno delle Maschere* (Naples, 1914).

3. R. Flatter, *The Moor of Venice* (1950).

4. B. Spivack, *Shakespeare and the Allegory of Evil* (N.Y., 1958).

5. T. Niklaus, *Harlequin Phoenix* (1956), p. 34.

6. K. M. Lea, *Italian Popular Comedy* (Oxford, 1934), II, 378–9.

7. A. Nicoll, *The World of Harlequin* (Cambridge, 1963), pp. 95–6.

8. See M. Esslin, *The Theatre of the Absurd* (1962), p. 212.

THOMAS RYMER AND *OTHELLO*

BY

NIGEL ALEXANDER

Rymer's celebrated critique of *Othello* contains a large number of difficult and important problems. It is part of a European critical debate about the nature of drama and it was this debate, dormant in England for over a hundred years, that T. S. Eliot was trying to revive when he remarked, in the course of one of his essays, 'I have never, by the way, seen a cogent refutation of Thomas Rymer's objections to *Othello*'.[1] Eliot saw the importance of the debate but his own remarks rather conceal the problem. Without saying that he himself considers the objections valid he leaves his reader to assume that objections which were first published in 1692/3 and have not yet been answered, must be fairly damaging. As Rymer's most recent editor, Curt A. Zimansky, says:

His attack on *Othello* remains a challenge since the attacks on probability seem valid and the play does raise special problems of moral and decorum.[2]

If Rymer's views are an important part of a vital critical argument it is essential to understand exactly what the argument is about.

The Tragedies of the Last Age and *A Short View of Tragedy* are among the fundamental critical texts which established neo-Aristotelian theories of art in England. Other critics, including Sidney and Jonson, had held these views before Rymer and other critical theories existed and caused acrimonious debate. But no critic in England had ever equalled Rymer in the rigour of his opinions or in his determination to follow the argument wherever it led—even if it led to the complete condemnation of English literature. Even when his opponents disagreed with his conclusions, and very few have ever actually admitted to agreeing with Rymer, they were in a difficult position. Despite his conclusions they seldom doubted the authority of the rules of art as expounded by the French and Italian commentators on Aristotle and apparently exemplified in the practice of the French dramatists. Consequently, since they accepted his premises, even critics like Charles Gildon and John Dennis, who began by producing extremely hostile 'answers' to Rymer, ended by accepting his critical methods. Dryden scribbled the *Heads of an Answer to Rymer* on the end papers of his copy of Rymer's book but in *The Grounds of Criticism in Tragedy* he felt bound to acknowledge:

How defective Shakespeare and Fletcher have been in all their plots, Mr Rymer has discovered in his criticisms.[3]

Dryden is not necessarily being inconsistent. If he agreed that Shakespeare was sometimes 'defective' in the art of his plots he continued to argue that he was a great poet by 'nature'.

It is exactly this debate, the controversy between 'nature' and 'art', that Eliot was trying to revive. Its revival was necessary because the century after Dryden had seen the complete critical triumph of those who believed that 'originality' and 'spontaneity' were the only criteria for poetry. Edward Young's *Conjectures on Original Composition* are an extreme example of the 'nature' side of this controversy just as Rymer's writings are a rigorous example of 'art'. The misinterpretation of Wordsworth gave these views about 'nature' currency far into the nineteenth century and allowed Macaulay, in his essay on Boswell's *Life of Johnson*, to dismiss Rymer in parenthesis as the worst critic who ever lived. Rymer's arguments have, in fact, seldom been considered except by critics who shared all his premises or by critics who shared none of them. They have, in other words, never received the critical attention that they deserve and the lack of 'cogent refutation' is a measure of their neglect rather than their infallibility.

When critics like Eliot or Zimansky agree with Rymer that the plot of *Othello* is improbable they are usually thinking of his objections to the time scheme of the play. This is certainly a puzzling feature and it can hardly be denied, as Rymer points out, that

Michael Cassio came not from *Venice* in the Ship with *Desdemona*, nor till this Morning could be suspected of an opportunity with her. And 'tis now but Dinner time; yet the *Moor* complains of his Fore-head. He might have set a Guard on *Cassio*, or have lockt up *Desdemona*, or have observ'd their carriage a day or two longer. He is on other occasions phlegmatick enough: this is very hasty.[4]

Shakespeare himself was clearly very well aware of this objection since he specifically makes Iago mention the period of betrothal as the likely beginning of the affair:

> *Iago*: Did Michael Cassio, when you wooed my lady,
> Know of your love? (III, iii, 94–5)

The action of the play appears to occupy at least three days, at most one week, and even if this is time for Othello's jealousy to develop, it is hardly sufficient for there to have been any cause for it. It is, however, precisely Shakespeare's point that within that time Othello can come to regard Desdemona as:

> that cunning whore of Venice
> That married with Othello. (IV, ii, 88–9)

Rymer, admitting that this is Shakespeare's point, argues that it is neither proper nor convincing. He does however try to strengthen his own case by arguing that in III, iv both Desdemona and Emilia talk as if the marriage had lasted for some years. Rymer suggests seven years but he is surely deceived by the fact that Emilia is clearly drawing upon her own experience in order to advise her mistress.

The lack of occasion for adultery would be an objection if time were one of the vital questions of the play. In *Hamlet*, for example, no audience can escape having the month that separated the funeral from the wedding forced upon their attention. In order to determine the time scheme of *Othello* it is necessary to go through the text with pencil and paper. The reason is simple and not difficult to accept. Gertrude's adultery is one of the vital questions of *Hamlet*, but Desdemona's adultery is not a question that is even raised in *Othello*. Indeed if the play is to have any point there must be no question whatsoever about her guilt or innocence. If the audience are to concentrate their attention on the important questions that the play does ask, they must not, at any stage, be debating whether Desdemona did or did not spend an afternoon naked in bed with Michael Cassio. Consequently the adultery is literally impossible and this, although Rymer did not realise it, is an extremely interesting example of the Aristotelian principle that a likely impossibility is to be preferred to an unlikely probability. This impossibility can be justified in dramatic terms provided that it can be shown that it allows the dramatist to direct the attention of the audience to more important matters. Here Rymer's criticism is both interesting and instructive because his objection to the time scheme is only a very minor part of his attack upon the play. His objections are a frontal assault upon all the major questions raised by the play and, since Rymer was an intelligent and competent neo-classic critic, his attack allows anyone who is prepared to follow his arguments and examine the play to distinguish the problems and determine the matter for themselves.

Rymer has four major objections to *Othello*. He declares that the marriage between Othello and Desdemona is itself improbable and monstrous. He denies that the characters in the play behave in any way like the soldiers or aristocrats of the Venetian Republic they are supposed to represent. He describes the whole episode of the handkerchief as absurd and, finally he asserts that Shakespeare's language is vulgar, mean and entirely beneath the dignity of tragedy. For the purpose of this study I intend to assume that Rymer has already been sufficiently answered when he writes:

In the *Neighing* of an Horse, or in the *growling* of a Mastiff, there is a meaning, there is as lively expression, and, may I say, more humanity, than many times in the Tragical flights of *Shakespear*.[5]

It is, in any case, only possible to discuss whether or not Shakespeare's language is appropriate to the situation after we have examined the situation. Such an examination involves a consideration of Rymer's first three objections which he claims to base upon the authority of both Aristotle and Horace. He was obviously thinking of Aristotle's *Poetics* 1450 b 21 and 1451 b 27 when he wrote in *The Tragedies of the Last Age*:

I have chiefly consider'd the *Fable* or *Plot*, which all conclude to be the *Soul* of a *Tragedy*; which, with the *Ancients*, is always found to be a *reasonable Soul*; but *with us*, for the most part, a *brutish*, and often worse than *brutish*.[6]

It is not, therefore, surprising that he begins his critique of *Othello* in *A Short View of Tragedy* with an account of the plot.

Rymer, however, has improved upon Aristotle in at least one respect. He believes that a play should not only have a plot but a moral as well. He is particularly sarcastic about the moral of *Othello*:

What ever rubs or difficulty may stick on the Bark, the Moral, sure, of this Fable is very instructive.
  1. First, This may be a caution to all Maidens of Quality how, without their Parents consent, they run away with Blackamoors.
  Di non si accompagnare con huomo, cui la natura & il cielo, & il modo della vita, disgiunge da noi. Cinthio.
  Secondly, This may be a warning to all good Wives, that they look well to their Linnen.
  Thirdly, This may be a lesson to Husbands, that before their Jealousie be Tragical, the proofs may be Mathematical.[7]

Rymer obviously feels that few of his countrymen stand in need of these exhortations. His point is that the moral of this play is improbably trivial because the whole plot and basis of the play, the love between Othello and Desdemona, is not merely improbable but unnatural and disgusting.

This match might well be without the Parents Consent. Old *Horace* long ago forbad the Banes.[8]

In order to make such a marriage either credible or presentable on the public stage, Rymer feels that the dramatist ought to suggest some special reason for Desdemona's strange tastes:

A little preparation and forecast might do well now and then. For his *Desdemona's* Marriage, He might have helped out the probability by feigning how that some way, or other, a Black-amoor Woman had been her Nurse, and suckl'd her: Or that once, upon a time, some *Virtuoso* had transfus'd into her Veins the Blood of a black Sheep: after which she might never be at quiet till she is, as the Poet will have it, *Tupt with an old black ram.*[9]

Rymer, however, has omitted to observe that Shakespeare has made use of exactly the 'preparation and forecast' that he recommends in order to help out the probability. Brabantio, like Rymer, cannot believe that his daughter would love Othello except through magical or chemical means and Othello defends himself against this charge before the Venetian senate:

> She loved me for the dangers I had passed,
> And I loved her that she did pity them.
> This only is the witchcraft I have used.
> Here comes the lady. Let her witness it. (I, iii, 166–9)

Rymer finds this whole scene and Othello's account of his wooing ridiculous and unnatural:

This was the Charm, this was the philtre, the love-powder that took the Daughter of this Noble Venetian. This was sufficient to make the Black-amoor White, and reconcile all, tho' there had been a Cloven-foot into the bargain.[10]

Anyone who does not believe Othello has to disbelieve the Doge as well. Rymer counters his line, 'I think this tale would win my daughter too', by quoting Horace's *Ars Poetica* lines 114–18:

Horace tells us,

> Intererit Multum...
> Colchus an Assyrius, Thebis nutritus, an Argis.[11]

and he goes on to argue that Othello's race and colour would have prevented his employment as a general in the service of the Venetian Republic:

The Character of that State is to employ strangers in their Wars; But shall a Poet thence fancy that they will set a Negro to be their General; or trust a *Moor* to defend them against the *Turk*? With us a Black-amoor might rise to be a Trumpeter; but *Shakespear* would not have him less than a Lieutenant-General. With us a *Moor* might marry some little drab, or Small-coal Wench: *Shakespear*, would provide him the Daughter and Heir of some great Lord, or Privy-Councellor: And all the Town should reckon it a very suitable match: Yet the English are not bred up with that hatred and aversion to the *Moors*, as are the Venetians, who suffer by a perpetual Hostility from them,

> Littora littoribus contraria...

Nothing is more odious in Nature than an improbable lye; And, certainly, never was any Play fraught, like this of *Othello*, with improbabilities.[12]

The conduct of the senators, in even listening to Othello's speech, is even more improbable than their employment of him as a general:

Instead of starting at the Prodigy, every one is familiar with *Desdemona*, as he were her own natural Father, rejoice in her good fortune, and wish their own several Daughters as hopefully married. Should the Poet have provided such a Husband for an only Daughter of any noble Peer in *England*, the Blackamoor must have chang'd his Skin to look our House of Lords in the Face.[13]

This is a familiar prejudice but one, apparently, which Shakespeare did not share. His development from Aaron the Moor in *Titus Andronicus* to Othello, the Moor of Venice, is a dramatic education in kinds of imagined villainy. It would be ironic if Rymer's attack was unanswerable because critics were incapable of profiting from that education.

Shakespeare, however, not only allows for Rymer's prejudice in his play: he founds his dramatic situation upon the gulf of race and custom which separates Othello from Desdemona. This gulf provides Iago with his opportunity:

> *Iago*: My lord, I see y'are moved.
> *Othello*:   No, not much moved.
> I do not think but Desdemona's honest.
> *Iago*: Long live she so. And long live you to think so.
> *Othello*: And yet, how nature erring from itself—
> *Iago*: Ay, there's the point, as (to be bold with you)
> Not to affect many proposed matches
> Of her own clime, complexion, and degree,
> Whereto we see in all things nature tends—
> Foh! one may smell in such a will most rank,
> Foul disproportion, thoughts unnatural.   (III, iii, 224–33)

There is, in *Othello*, as great a disagreement about the use of the word 'natural' as there is in *Hamlet*. In calling Desdemona 'unnatural' Iago expresses the crass, the vulgar view of her marriage. This is a point of view which carries death and destruction with it and is liable, at any period of history, to involve mankind in fatal and tragic action. In *Othello* tragic action develops and becomes possible when Othello comes to share this vulgar view of his own marriage—the view which is also held by Thomas Rymer. Rymer quotes Iago's speech and comments:

The Poet here is certainly in the right, and by consequence the foundation of the Play must be concluded to be Monstrous; And the constitution, all over, to be *most rank*,
> *Foul disproportion, thoughts unnatural.*
Which instead of moving pity, or any passion Tragical and Reasonable, can produce nothing but horror and aversion, and what is odious and grievous to an Audience.[14]

This, then, is one of the objections which so far lacks cogent refutation.

Rymer's own prejudice prevents him from seeing that the dramatist has deliberately used this prejudice, expressed by Iago, Brabantio and Roderigo, as part of his play and that, within the play, he has also provided an answer to it. Desdemona herself answers Rymer's objection:

> My heart's subdued
> Even to the very quality of my lord.
> I saw Othello's visage in his mind.   (I, iii, 245–7)

The Duke adopts this answer for himself before the end of the scene.

> And, noble signior,
> If virtue no delighted beauty lack,
> Your son-in-law is far more fair than black. (I, iii, 283–5)

Rymer, of course, does not believe this answer. What he does not see is that whether he does, or does not believe it, is quite irrelevant to his critical view of the play. *Othello* does not present its audience with only one view of the central marriage. It combines many opposed views in order to present a series of difficult questions. Desdemona sees Othello's visage in his mind and does not use the intellectual arts which even Emilia employs in dealing with her husband. The audience are invited to compare and contrast their attitudes to marriage. Since the nature of the marriage is difficult and unusual, Othello can be brought to believe Iago's view of it. The audience are asked to consider Iago's views very carefully. The marriage, and its difficulties, are the foundation, as Rymer says, upon which the play is built. The fact that it is possible for men like Iago, or even men like Rymer, to consider such a marriage 'monstrous' makes the ensuing catastrophe necessary and probable. Shakespeare has incorporated such a view into his play in order to explain the fierce blaze of Othello's self-destructive jealousy which might, in other circumstances, seem excessive or unnatural. At the end of the scene in the senate the future course of the play's action is predicted in four lines:

> *Brabantio:* Look to her, Moor, if thou hast eyes to see:
> She has deceived her father, and may thee.
> *Othello:* My life upon her faith! Honest Iago,
> My Desdemona must I leave to thee. (I, iii, 287–90)

The result of such a trust is already apparent by III, iii, 206 as Iago begins to insinuate his, and Brabantio's view of the marriage into Othello's mind, 'She did deceive her father, marrying you'. Yet, although he accepts this view for a time, Othello will, by the end of the play, sacrifice his life upon Desdemona's faith. Rymer, therefore, correctly describes the marriage as the foundation of the play but his prejudice prevents him from observing that the play dramatizes the great leap of faith and love that such a marriage requires. The play leaves its audience with a question but there are more answers to it than are dreamt of in Rymer's philosophy.

To do Rymer justice, however, it is important to notice that he is blinded by critical as well as personal considerations. Any view of the marriage must be presented through the characters and Rymer regards them as equally monstrous and improbable. He is not, therefore, likely to listen with much patience to their explanation. If the characters are indeed improbable then the dramatist is himself to blame if their views are received with scorn. It is Rymer's case that these characters are supposed to be soldiers and aristocrats and yet their words and actions bear no relation to the known conduct and proper bearing of either of these classes. As he says:

The *Characters* or Manners, which are the second part in a Tragedy, are not less unnatural and improper, than the Fable was improbable and absurd. *Othello* is made a Venetian General. We see nothing done by him, nor related concerning him, that comports with the condition of a General, or, indeed, of a Man, unless the killing himself, to avoid a death the Law was about to inflict upon him. When his Jealousy had wrought him up to a resolution of 's taking revenge for the suppos'd injury, He sets *Jago* to the fighting part, to kill *Cassio*; And chuses himself to murder the silly Woman his Wife, that was like to make no resistance. His Love and his Jealousie are no part of a Souldiers Character, unless for Comedy.

But what is most intolerable is *Jago*. He is no Black-amoor Souldier, so we may be sure he should be like other Souldiers of our acquaintance; yet never in Tragedy, nor in Comedy, nor in Nature was a Souldier with his Character.[15]

Rymer here fails in the critic's most important duty. He fails to give an exact and accurate account of the work that he is criticizing. The audience hears various opinions of Othello's generalship from the Venetian senate and from the garrison at Cyprus. Othello does not kill himself to avoid execution, but for the same reason that he chose to murder Desdemona—as an act of that 'poetical justice' which Rymer himself so often advocated. Rymer is similarly inaccurate when he criticizes the behaviour of the members of the Venetian senate:

They will sit up all night to hear a Doctors Commons, Matrimonial, Cause. And have the Merits of the Cause at large laid open to 'em, that they may decide it before they Stir. What can be pleaded to keep awake their attention so wonderfully?[16]

The senate, as Rymer is well aware, is engaged in taking desperate counter measures against a threatening Turkish fleet. In the middle of this preparation Othello, their selected commander, is accused of witchcraft. The Athenian assembly attempted to recall Alcibiades from the Sicilian expedition when he was accused of sacrilege. There are good classical precedents as well as probable reasons for the conduct of the Venetian senate who are certainly not sitting simply to hear a matrimonial cause.

To say, however, that Rymer is often inaccurate does not dispose of his charge that the character of Iago in particular is monstrous. This objection requires attention and careful consideration. Rymer argues that an audience will expect stage characters to conform to the 'typical' or 'natural' characteristics of the people they represent and that a dramatist who disappoints the reasonable expectation of an audience does not know his own business. As C. A. Zimansky points out this is not fundamentally an absurd or ludicrous view:

Specific applications of the idea are carried to extremes, but the whole concept requires examination before we too hastily condemn it as mere fantastic etiquette. There are certain characteristics belonging to a nationality, a class, an age group, or a profession; the 17th-century revival of the Theophrastan character is helpful but hardly necessary to illustrate the idea. Horace had, as a practical matter, advised his young poets to be observant of such characteristics. Or, as a present-day writer puts it, 'And just as behaviour should proceed from character so should speech. A fashionable woman should talk like a fashionable woman, a street walker like a street walker, a soda jerker like a soda jerker and a lawyer like a lawyer.'[17]

As Rymer points out, *Othello* is filled with military affairs. The idea and character of the soldier is clearly of vital importance for the play. Yet Shakespeare has created Iago in flagrant contradiction to all of a soldier's known or typical characteristics:

Shakespear knew his Character of *Jago* was inconsistent. In this very Play he pronounces,

> *If thou dost deliver more or less than Truth*
> *Thou art no Souldier.*

This he knew, but to entertain the Audience with something new and surprising, against common sense, and Nature, he would pass upon us a close, dissembling, false, insinuating rascal, instead of an open-hearted, frank, plain-dealing Souldier, a character constantly worn by them for some thousands of years in the World.[18]

Rymer then goes on to support this criticism by expanding Aristotle's observation that poetry is more philosophical than history:

Philosophy tells us it is a principle in the Nature of Man *to be grateful.*

   History may tell us that *John an Oaks, John a Stiles,* or *Jago* were ungrateful; *Poetry* is to follow Nature; Philosophy must be his guide: history and *fact* in particular cases of *John an Oaks,* or *John of Styles,* are no warrant or direction for a Poet. Therefore *Aristotle* is always telling us that Poetry is σπουδαιώτερον καὶ φιλοσοφώτερον, is more general and abstracted, is led more by the Philosophy, the reason and nature of things, than History: which only records things higlety, piglety, right or wrong as they happen. History might without any preamble or difficulty, say that *Jago* was ungrateful. Philosophy then calls him unnatural; But the Poet is not, without huge labour and preparation to expose the Monster; and after shew the Divine Vengeance executed upon him.[19]

Here Rymer fails to benefit from his own critical insight. It is certainly true that when Montano appeals to Iago after the affray on the court of guard:

> If partially affined, or leagued in office,
> Thou dost deliver more or less than truth,
> Thou art no soldier. (II, iii, 217–19)

he is appealing to precisely that 'character' of the honest soldier described by Rymer. But this appeal is itself part of the 'huge labour and preparation' which Shakespeare employs to prepare his audience for Iago. Unless the 'character' of the honest soldier existed, Shakespeare could not have created Iago. 'Honest Iago' is one of the phrases that rings perpetually throughout the play. The tragedy is made possible because all of the characters on stage believe Iago to be the pattern of the honest soldier described by Horace. Iago uses the language of honesty and the appearance of plain dealing to all the characters—only to the audience does he reveal his nature, which is in many respects the exact opposite of what he appears to be. As Jan Kott, and other critics before him, have pointed out, there are two languages in the play of *Othello*. One is full of terms of honour, trust and love. The other, spoken by Iago, is filled with images of bestiality and hatred. At the centre of the play Othello adopts Iago's language. When Othello leaves Lodovico, the representative of Venice, with the words 'Goats and monkeys' on his lips, Iago's triumph appears complete. His view of the world has won acceptance even from those it destroys.

   This view of the world is, as Rymer says, monstrous. It is, however, perfectly comprehensible. What Coleridge called the 'motive-hunting of a motiveless malignity' is, in fact, the dramatist's careful preparation of his character. Jealousy, Envy, Hatred and an obscure Lust pursue each other with increasing speed through Iago's mind. His intellect is dedicated to the service of these passions and they, therefore, dictate how he must employ his intellect. He achieves the consummation of his wishes through deceit and treachery. If this conduct appears horrible, it is because it is the opposite of the 'Philosophy' commended by Rymer, which states that it is the nature of man to be grateful. If it were not 'natural' for man to be grateful Iago's conduct could not appear 'unnatural'. The success of all Iago's schemes depends upon the fact that he is dealing with men and women of a free, open, honest and credulous disposition. The action of the play is based upon the open character of the soldier no less than on the unusual nature of the marriage. Shakespeare has merely proved himself rather better at applying the precepts of Horace and Aristotle than Rymer.

Iago's opportunity, for example, comes through Emilia's 'natural' desire to please her husband—a desire she betrays her mistress to satisfy, though the betrayal appears a trifling matter. She merely keeps a handkerchief which Desdemona had dropped. This handkerchief, however, proves the ruin and death of her mistress and Emilia then speaks out without fear of the death threatened to her by both Othello and Iago. The truth is now too late to save her mistress but it is not too late to destroy the language of Iago. He had used Othello's love for Desdemona to destroy them both but he had not considered that Emilia's love for Desdemona might destroy him. Iago's calculations, therefore, were incomplete because they had failed to allow for the virtue of Emilia. Rymer, however, considers it a fault that the dramatist allowed his calculations sufficient force to destroy Desdemona. Yet, in his examination of these events Rymer himself asks one of the central questions of the play:

Rather may we ask here what unnatural crime *Desdemona*, or her Parents had committed, to bring this Judgment down upon her; to Wed a Black-amoor, and innocent to be thus cruelly murder'd by him. What instruction can we make out of this Catastrophe? Or whither must our reflection lead us ? Is not this to envenome and sour our spirits, to make us repine and grumble at Providence; and the government of the World? If this be our end, what boots it to be Vertuous?[20]

Rymer's error, which he shares with many more highly respected critics, is to suppose that it is the business of the dramatist to understand the workings of Providence or the government of the world. Rymer admits that the accidents of history may obscure the divine order of the world and the operation of eternal justice. But because that order and justice certainly exist the poet, guided by philosophy, must represent them upon his stage. Sophocles and Euripides, according to Rymer, were the first poets to realise this:

They concluded, that a *Poet* must of necessity see *justice* exactly administered, if he intended to please.[21]

It is easy to pour scorn upon such an idea but it is more helpful to observe that 'poetical justice' certainly exists in *Othello*. Rymer has simply not realized the full implications of his own criticism. The author is not in a position to penetrate beyond the accidents of history but he can, and does, leave his audience with a question, 'If this be our end, what boots it to be Vertuous?' Neither the religion of Sophocles and Euripides nor the Christian religion promises immunity from trouble to the virtuous. Yet very few tragedies end with the complete and open triumph of the forces of evil and destruction. *Othello*, certainly, is not among them.

The instrument of 'poetical justice' in *Othello* is the very handkerchief which Rymer believes to be too trivial and mean a cause of the tragedy. He comments on Emilia's revelation that she found the handkerchief and gave it to Iago:

Here we see the meanest woman in the Play takes this *Handkerchief* for a *trifle* below her Husband to trouble his head about it. Yet we find, it entered into our Poets head, to make a Tragedy of this *Trifle*.[22]

It is, of course, precisely its apparent triviality that makes it important. If it had not appeared trivial Emilia would never have stolen it from her mistress. Even when she has stolen it and Othello's terrible jealousy is at work, she never suspects that this handkerchief could be its cause. Iago himself did not expect very much from it and only uses it as one scheme among many:

I will in Cassio's lodging lose this napkin
And let him find it. Trifles light as air
Are to the jealous confirmations strong
As proofs of Holy Writ. This may do something.

(III, iii, 318–21)

Iago, however, had not allowed for the value attached to the handkerchief by Othello. The fact that 'There's magic in the web of it' is something that could not have been foreseen. When she learns of this 'magic' Desdemona's obvious feelings of guilt at losing it and her righteous insistence upon her suit for Cassio are then construed by Othello as evidence of her love for Cassio. As it happens the handkerchief was not a trifle to Othello although it appears to be one to all the other characters in the play. It has now become the deadly instrument of Iago's witchcraft which uses Othello's whole personality as the spell for Desdemona's destruction. In wooing Desdemona, Othello had used no witchcraft but words. By the witchcraft of Iago's words she is destroyed and only when she is dead does Emilia realize that her husband is responsible, and speaks the exorcism which costs her life. In using the handkerchief, therefore, Iago was preparing his own destruction as well as Desdemona's. Iago falls a victim to his own plot just as Claudius, for example, dies by his own poison: both are examples of the true operation of 'poetical justice'.

Rymer, therefore, was an intelligent and competent neo-classic critic and his criticism is directed to the three vital questions of the play. These questions are the nature and validity of the marriage between Othello and Desdemona, the source and direction of Iago's terrifying power and the trifle of the handkerchief. They remain questions after the play is over, because, despite the leap of love and faith, the marriage was vulnerable to attack—an attack which is not finally or 'ultimately' explained since Iago defends himself with silence. It is because these questions remain to puzzle the will that *Othello* continues to exercise its power over the imagination. The dramatist has not solved the differences which divide mankind or solved the problem of evil, but the very violence of Rymer's reaction is a testimony to the power with which these problems have been dramatized. What confuses the issue is that, although Rymer was an acute critic, he was also convinced that he knew the answers to all the questions raised by the play and his analysis is therefore accompanied by a great deal of ethical dogmatism which can now only appear comic. The questions have outlasted Rymer's answers and the play has survived his criticism because Shakespeare had incorporated these answers in the structure of *Othello*. The success of the play in provoking Rymer to expose his own beliefs on these questions should warn other critics that the play acts as a mirror up to nature for its audience as well as for the characters on stage.

In *The Tragedies of the Last Age* Rymer was aware that some of his objections to *A King and No King* might equally be applied to Greek drama. His defence is reasonable and a model of dramatic criticism:

I know with the Ancients, *Orestes* kill'd his Mother, *Hercules* his Wife and Children, *Agamemnon* his Daughter. But the first was an act of *Justice*; the second of *Frenzy*; the last of *Religion*. But these were all Tragedies unhappy in the *catastrophe*. And the business so well prepar'd; that every one might see, that these Worthies had rather have laid violent hands on themselves, had not their *will* and choice been over-rul'd. Every step they made, appear'd so contrary to their inclinations, as all the while shew'd them unhappy, and render'd them the most *deserving* of pitty in the World.[23]

Othello, his will and choice over-ruled by the terrible power of Iago, kills Desdemona as an act of Justice, although it could also be described as an act of Frenzy. When he realizes what he has done he does, as an act of Religion, lay violent hands upon himself. Rymer failed to see that Shakespeare, like Sophocles, had prepared his business well because the play of *Othello* raised questions which Rymer found 'unthinkable'. They are, however, questions which have to be faced and which must be answered as men go about their business in this century. Eliot, therefore, is incorrect when he says that he had never seen a cogent refutation of Rymer. He had most certainly read at least one, for it was written by William Shakespeare and it is called *Othello, the Moor of Venice*.

© R. N. ALEXANDER 1968

NOTES

1. T. S. Eliot, 'Hamlet', *Selected Essays 1917–1932* (1932), p. 141.

2. Curt A. Zimansky, Introduction to *The Critical Works of Thomas Rymer* (New Haven, 1956), p. li.

3. John Dryden, 'The Grounds of Criticism in Tragedy', *Essays of John Dryden*, ed. W. P. Ker (Oxford, 1900), I, 211.

4. Zimansky, *Rymer*, 'A Short View of Tragedy', p. 150.

5. *Ibid.* p. 136.

6. Zimansky, *Rymer*, 'Tragedies of the Last Age', p. 18.

7. Zimansky, *Rymer*, 'A Short View of Tragedy', p. 132.

8. *Ibid.* p. 132.

9. *Ibid.* p. 167.

10. *Ibid.* p. 133.

11. *Ibid.* p. 133.

12. *Ibid.* p. 134.

13. *Ibid.* p. 139

14. *Ibid.* p. 150.

15. *Ibid.* p. 134.

16. *Ibid.* p. 138.

17. Zimansky, Introduction to *Rymer*, p. xxv, quoting Somerset Maugham, 'What Makes a Good Novel Great,' *New York Times Book Review*, 30 November 1947, p. i.

18. Zimansky, *Rymer*, 'A Short View of Tragedy', p. 135.

19. *Ibid.* p. 163. Aristotle actually describes poetry as φιλοσοφώτερον καὶ σπουδαιότερον.

20. Zimansky, *Rymer*, 'A Short View of Tragedy', p. 161.

21. Zimansky, *Rymer*, 'Tragedies of the Last Age', p. 22.

22. Zimansky, *Rymer*, 'A Short View of Tragedy', p. 163.

23. Zimansky, *Rymer*, 'Tragedies of the Last Age', p. 48.